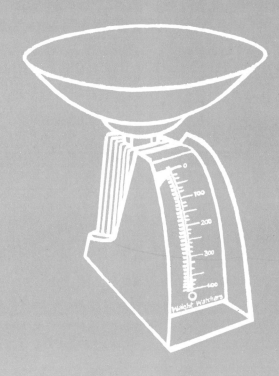

The illustration on the front cover shows a dinner party for two: spaghetti with tomato sauce, beef stroganoff with vegetables and salad and lemon strawberry foam.

CONTENTS

INTRODUCTION

This is a book about cooking and eating almost every delicious food you care to think of.
Believe it or not, it is a book especially written for fat people.
Surely, eating is the one thing fat people should *not* do? Far from it. Eating is the only way there is to get slim and *stay* slim, FOREVER.
If you are a member of Weight Watchers, this will be nothing new to you. If you are not, you may raise your eyebrows and think what an extraordinary idea it is.
But there is nothing revolutionary about it.
In fact British Weight Watchers have been practising it for the last five years, ever since they opened their first class in a tiny village in Buckinghamshire.
It worked then and it works now. To prove it there are in Britain today thousands of former fatties who have already become, or are learning to become, permanently slim people. There are millions more men, women and children throughout the world who have practised this same eat-to-stay-slim system and found it did exactly that for them, too.
How is it Weight Watchers can make this unusual idea work? Firstly, you must realise one thing. It is not food itself that makes you fat.
It is the overwhelming compulsion to eat incorrect quantities of those foods which do.
Diets, pills, injections and other slimming treatments are not only unpleasant to experience, but the results are short-lived. Before you can say Billy Bunter you will be back on the old bad habits and in need of another tortuous diet.
Weight Watchers is none of these. It is a sensible easy-to-follow Programme of Eating that works—and keeps on working throughout your life. It shows you how to lose weight sensibly and safely and keep it off.
Weight Watchers get right down to the root of the problem—those bad eating habits which are both your downfall and your girth. At weekly classes trained lecturers teach you a new pattern of eating which is presented in the Programme of Eating.
The going is far from tough, even in this initial period when you are going all out to reduce to the goal weight which is assessed according to life assurance company tables. You never go hungry. The Programme sees to that. Unlike dieters, you can eat three square meals a day and always have a variety of satisfying, interesting food in front of you. The photographs in this book illustrate just how well you can eat.
You attend meetings and follow the Programme until you are well on the way to achieving your goal weight. Then you start on the Levelling Programme which helps to prevent any demoralising plateau before achieving goal.
On achieving goal, you go on the Maintenance Plan which allows most of those foods and drinks you have craved and missed. Only by now, of course, you won't be craving them as much as you thought you would. The Programme of Eating will have already established a sensibly balanced control over your mind and your senses.
Why attend classes? Why not give fat people the Programme and let them get on with it?
One of the main reasons for Weight Watchers success is the classes. This is because most fat people cannot learn to re-educate their eating patterns on their own. However much they try, they find it almost impossible not to cheat.
A temptation shared is a temptation halved. That is how the group therapy works. Alone they lose but together they win, backed by the moral support of fellow members who share with them the one common interest and objective of getting slim and staying slim.
If they do cheat, they know they will have to confess at the next meeting. That in itself is a strong deterrent.
Weight Watchers introduced a New Programme of Eating, January 1972. Based on the most advanced medical and scientific research carried out by internationally-known doctors and dieticians, it has been adapted to suit our British tastes and habits.
This Programme means that as a member of Weight Watchers you need never go hungry. Now you can eat rice, spaghetti, even potatoes— and still lose weight, always provided the right balance and prescribed amounts are observed. The new Programme, with its inclusion of satisfying foods formerly considered fattening, now makes your goal weight even more readily accessible than before. The eight-week Maintenance Plan is now a carefully supervised course for returning formerly forbidden foods to your normal way of life. Chocolate cake, jam, gin and whisky are all in this Plan, and you can

learn to enjoy them normally and still stay slim. This book in itself is no magic passport to being slim. Only Weight Watchers can help you do that. However, you will be able to enjoy the recipes here in the happy knowledge that, unlike most other gourmet recipes, they will not *make* you fat.

Whether you are fat or thin, a former member of Weight Watchers or a future one, eat and eat and stay slim.

RECIPE INSTRUCTIONS

Weight Watchers—please read before preparing recipes.

If you are preparing more than one course, check recipes carefully to ensure that you are not exceeding your meal time or daily allowance of limited foods.

All gelatine used must be unflavoured.

One slice of bread shall be no more than one ounce in weight.

Dishes containing fish, meat or poultry: these when prepared according to the recipe will meet the exact Weight Watchers meal time allowances. However, it is still a very good idea to weigh your food after cooking.

The weights given for fish, meat or poultry in dinner recipes are the permitted allowance for ladies. The number of portions are indicated at either the top or foot of the recipe. Men must increase their dinner time allowance of fish, meat or poultry according to their requirements.

Note to Non-Weight Watchers.

Daily allowances, limited and non-limited foods, and legal and illegal foods are fully explained in the Weight Watchers Programme of Eating which is available only to registered members of Weight Watchers.

With the exception of some soups, sauces, vegetables/salads, desserts and drinks which may be eaten and drunk for lunch or dinner, all recipes are marked Breakfast, Lunch or Dinner, according to the meal at which they should be eaten.

SOUPS

Soup is a delicious way of using your daily vegetable allowance. When you are entertaining and want to provide your guests with a 3-course meal, serve a vegetable soup as a starter—it is a good way of fitting in an extra course without breaking the rules.
Many soups taste just as good cold as they do hot, especially in summer. Brighten up dull-coloured soups with a garnish of a contrasting colour, such as chopped parsley or chives, finely diced red and green peppers and celery, or a sprig of watercress. Toasted (not fried) croûtons go well with many soups, but remember to take this out of the permitted bread allowance.
If you are going in for soup-making, a blender is an essential piece of kitchen equipment.

BORTSCH

Serves One

4 oz. cooked lean beef
1 oz. leek
1 oz. carrot
1 oz. onion
1 stick celery
⅛ small cabbage
1 pint beef stock made with beef stock cube and water
4 small mushrooms
1 bay leaf
¼ teaspoon dried thyme
1 clove garlic, crushed (optional)
salt and pepper
1 oz. cooked beetroot
lemon juice

Chop the beef into small pieces. Dice the leek, carrot, onion and celery. Shred the cabbage finely. Place the meat, prepared vegetables and stock in a saucepan. Bring to the boil, cover and simmer for 15 minutes.
Wash and chop the mushrooms. Add them to the saucepan with the bay leaf, thyme and garlic. Season to taste. Continue cooking for 10 minutes. Remove the bay leaf.
Grate the beetroot and sprinkle with a little lemon juice.
Stir the beetroot into the soup, just before serving.

CAULIFLOWER AND TOMATO SOUP

Serves Four

1 small cauliflower
½ pint tomato juice
¾ pint chicken stock made with chicken stock cube and water
salt and pepper
4 oz. button mushrooms
1 teaspoon dried basil
1 tablespoon chopped parsley

Wash the cauliflower, including the outside green leaves. Cut it into small pieces and place in a saucepan with the tomato juice, stock, salt and pepper. Bring to the boil, cover the pan and simmer for about 15 minutes or until the cauliflower is very tender. Cool.

Chop the mushrooms and place them in an electric blender with the cauliflower and the cooking liquid. Blend at high speed until smooth. Return to the saucepan, add the basil, bring to the boil again and simmer for 3 minutes. Taste and adjust seasoning.
Stir in the parsley just before serving.
Note: To make this into a cream soup, add 3 teaspoons skimmed milk powder to each serving of the soup.

COUNTRY SOUP

Serves One

1 teaspoon dried onion flakes
½ pint chicken stock made with chicken stock cube and water
4 small mushrooms
6 tablespoons tomato juice
salt and pepper
4 oz. cooked elbow macaroni

Place the onion flakes in a saucepan with the chicken stock, bring to the boil and simmer until onion flakes are softened. Chop the mushrooms and add to the pan with the tomato juice, salt and pepper to taste. Bring to the boil and simmer for 10 minutes.
Stir in macaroni and reheat.

CREAM OF CELERY SOUP

Serves Two

1 head celery
2 beef or chicken stock cubes
¾ pint hot water
1–2 tablespoons skimmed milk powder

Wash the celery thoroughly and chop coarsely. Dissolve the stock cubes in the water and pour into a saucepan. Add the celery, bring to the boil, cover the pan and simmer until celery is very tender.
Either place the soup in an electric blender and blend at high speed until smooth or beat very well until smooth.
Return the soup to the saucepan, stir in the milk powder and reheat, stirring, without boiling.

CREAM OF ONION SOUP

Serves One

$\frac{1}{4}$ pint skimmed milk
4 oz. chopped onion
$\frac{1}{4}$ pint chicken stock made with chicken stock cube and
water

Put all ingredients into a saucepan. Bring to the
boil, stirring, then simmer, covered, for about
20 minutes or until the onion is very tender.
Serve very hot.

CURRY SOUP

Serves Two

$\frac{3}{4}$ pint chicken stock made with chicken stock cube and
water
5 oz. cauliflower
$\frac{1}{3}$ teaspoon curry powder
chopped parsley for garnish

Put the chicken stock into a saucepan with the
cauliflower. Bring to the boil, cover the pan and
simmer until the cauliflower is very tender.
Add the curry powder 2–3 minutes before the
cooking time is completed.

Bortsch (above)
Hungarian Thick Soup (opposite)

Pour the soup into an electric blender and
blend on the highest speed until smooth.
Serve hot, sprinkled with chopped parsley.

HUNGARIAN THICK SOUP

Serves Four

1×1 lb. 3 oz. can celery hearts
4 oz. button mushrooms
1 pint chicken stock made with chicken stock cube and
water
2 teaspoons paprika pepper
$\frac{1}{4}$ teaspoon dried tarragon
salt and pepper

Place celery hearts and liquid in blender and
blend at high speed until smooth.
Alternatively, mash very well with a fork.
Slice the mushrooms and combine with stock,
paprika, tarragon, salt and pepper and simmer
until mushrooms are tender, add blended
celery hearts, bring to boil and simmer for 2–3
minutes, taste and adjust seasoning, serve hot.

10

LEMON CHICKEN SOUP

Serves Two

¾ pint chicken stock made with chicken stock cube and
 water
2 oz. mushrooms
1 tablespoon chopped parsley
8 oz. cooked elbow macaroni
2 teaspoons fresh lemon juice

Place the chicken stock in a saucepan. Wash the
mushrooms, slice thinly and add to the saucepan
with the chopped parsley. Bring to the boil and
simmer for a few minutes until the mushrooms
are tender. Add the cooked macaroni and reheat.
Remove the saucepan from the heat and stir in
the lemon juice.

ITALIAN EGG SOUP   Lunch

Serves One

12 fl. oz. chicken stock made with chicken stock cube
 and water
1 teaspoon chopped parsley
1 tablespoon tomato juice
1 egg
pinch of pepper
salt to taste
1 oz. grated Cheddar cheese

Place the stock in a saucepan with the parsley
and tomato juice. Bring to the boil and simmer
for 1 minute.
Beat the egg and pepper together. Add to the
simmering stock and cook, stirring, for
2–3 seconds. Add salt if necessary.
Pour into a serving bowl and sprinkle the grated
cheese on top. Serve at once.

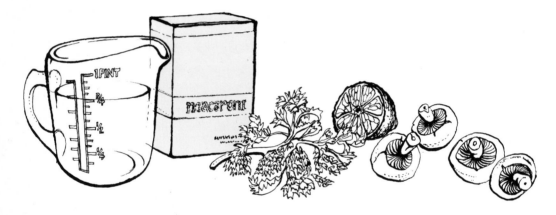

LETTUCE AND CELERY SOUP

Serves Four

8 oz. celery
onion salt to taste
1 blade mace
1½ pints chicken stock made with chicken stock
 cubes and water
1 small lettuce
salt and pepper
chopped parsley for garnish

Chop the celery and place in a saucepan with the
onion salt, mace and chicken stock. Bring to the
boil, cover pan and simmer until the celery is
tender. Press through a sieve into a clean
saucepan.
Shred the lettuce and add to the pan. Bring to
the boil again and simmer for a further 10
minutes. Taste and adjust seasoning.
Serve piping hot, sprinkled with chopped
parsley.

THICK TOMATO SOUP

Serves Two to Three

2 chicken stock cubes
4 fl. oz. hot water
12 fl. oz. tomato juice
2 teaspoons dried onion flakes
1 lb. marrow
pepper
few drops artificial liquid sweetener (optional)

Crumble the stock cubes into the water and stir
to dissolve. Place in a large saucepan and add the
tomato juice, onion flakes and the peeled, cored
and diced marrow. Bring to the boil, cover the
pan and simmer gently for about 20 minutes or
until the marrow is very tender.
Pour the soup into an electric blender and blend
at high speed until smooth. Return soup to the
pan and reheat. Taste and adjust seasoning.
Serve piping hot.

TOMATO AND BEANSPROUT SOUP

Serves Two

1 stick celery
1 pint chicken stock made with chicken stock cube and
water
1 × 16 oz. can bean sprouts
¼ pint tomato juice
few sprigs of cauliflower
¼ teaspoon mixed spice
salt and pepper
3 drops artificial liquid sweetener
6 oz. cooked star noodles or other small pasta

Cut the celery into 1 inch lengths and place in a
saucepan with the chicken stock, drained and
rinsed bean sprouts, tomato juice, cauliflower,
spice, salt and pepper. Bring to the boil, stirring
occasionally, cover the pan and simmer for
1 hour.
Stir in the sweetener and cooked noodles,
reheat gently.

WATERCRESS SOUP

Serves One

1 bunch watercress
½ pint chicken stock made with chicken stock cube and
water
1 tablespoon skimmed milk powder
freshly ground black pepper

Wash the watercress, cut off bottom third of the
stems and chop the remainder. Place the
watercress in a saucepan with the stock. Bring to
the boil and simmer for 10 minutes. Pour into an
electric blender and blend at high speed until
smooth. Pour back into the saucepan, stir in the
skimmed milk powder, add pepper and reheat
without boiling. Serve either piping hot or
chilled, garnished with sprigs of watercress.

WEIGHT WATCHERS ALL-IN SOUP

Serves Four

2 heaped tablespoons shredded white cabbage
1 stick celery, chopped
1 small cauliflower, chopped
2 oz. courgettes, sliced
1 oz. mushrooms, chopped
1½ pints water
1 bay leaf
½ teaspoon dried dill
1 clove garlic, crushed (optional)
1 beef stock cube, crumbled
salt

Place all the ingredients together in a large
saucepan. Bring to the boil, cover the pan and
simmer gently for about 45 minutes or until all
the vegetables are well cooked. Remove the
bay leaf.
Taste and adjust the seasoning. Either serve as it
is, piping hot, or pour into an electric blender
and blend at high speed until smooth. Reheat
before serving.

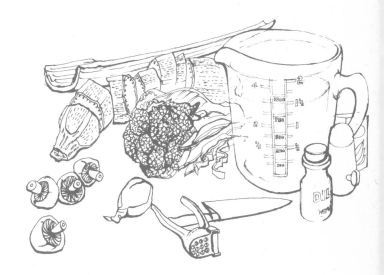

WINTER SOUP

Serves Two

½ pint tomato juice
½ beef stock cube
1 teaspoon chopped mint
2 teaspoons chopped parsley
salt and pepper
¼ teaspoon Worcestershire sauce
artificial liquid sweetener to equal 2 teaspoons sugar
4 oz. finely shredded cabbage
2 sticks celery
2 bunches watercress
¼ box mustard and cress

Place the tomato juice in a saucepan with the
stock cube, mint, parsley, salt and pepper,
Worcestershire sauce and sweetener. Bring to the
boil, stirring occasionally. Add the cabbage and
the remaining vegetables, all cleaned and
chopped. Bring to the boil again, cover the pan
and simmer gently for 10–15 minutes or until
the vegetables are just tender.
Taste and adjust seasoning. Serve as it is,
a hearty soup, or thin down with water if
preferred and reheat.

13

Watercress Soup (opposite)

Jellied Grapefruit Consommé (bottom right)

Gazpacho (bottom left)

GAZPACHO

Serves Three

2 tomatoes
1 green pepper
1 stick celery
1 tablespoon dried onion flakes
½ cucumber
¼ pint chicken stock made from chicken stock cube and
    water
12 fl. oz. tomato juice
1 clove garlic, crushed
2 tablespoons cider vinegar
salt and pepper

Plunge the tomatoes in boiling water for
1 minute, rinse in cold water and remove the
skins. Remove the pips and seeds from the pepper
and chop finely. Chop the tomatoes and celery.
Soak the onion flakes until softened. Peel the
cucumber and chop roughly. Place the celery,
tomato, ¼ of the pepper and ½ the onion flakes
in a small bowl and reserve.
Place all the remaining vegetables in an electric
blender with the stock, tomato juice, garlic,
vinegar and salt and pepper. Blend all together
at high speed until smooth, about 2 minutes.
Chill the soup before serving. Serve sprinkled
with the reserved vegetable garnish.

SUMMER FRUIT SOUP

Serves Three

3 cooking apples or ripe pears
3 peaches
1½ pints water
2 lemons
2 teaspoons skimmed milk powder
artificial sweetener to taste
1–2 teaspoons ground cinnamon
slices of lemon and watercress for garnish

Peel and core the apples or pears. Skin the
peaches. Slice all the fruit, retain the peach
stones as these add flavour to the soup.
Put the fruit into a saucepan with the water and
lemon rinds. Bring to the boil, cover the pan
and simmer until the fruit is soft. Press the fruit
through a sieve and return to the saucepan.
Mix the milk powder with the lemon juice and
stir into the soup. Bring to the boil and simmer,
uncovered, for a further 15 minutes until
thickened. Stir in the sweetener and cinnamon.
Chill well and serve garnished with slices of
lemon and sprigs of watercress.

JELLIED GRAPEFRUIT CONSOMMÉ

Serves Two

juice of 1 grapefruit
scant ½ oz. gelatine
artificial sweetener to taste
¼ cucumber
salt and freshly ground black pepper
chopped mint for garnish

Pour the grapefruit juice into a measuring jug
and make up to ¾ pint with cold water. Pour
into a saucepan, sprinkle on the gelatine and
heat gently, stirring constantly, until the
gelatine has dissolved. Sweeten to taste. Chill the
mixture until syrupy and beginning to set.
Chop the cucumber and stir into the grapefruit
with salt and pepper to taste. Leave in a cool
place until firm and set.
Chop the jelly and spoon into 2 serving dishes.
Serve sprinkled with chopped mint leaves.

JELLIED VEGETABLE HORS D'OEUVRE

Serves Four to Five

8 oz. courgettes
½ teaspoon salt
freshly ground black pepper
1 red pepper
½ cucumber
chopped parsley
scant ½ oz. gelatine
½ pint tomato juice
1 teaspoon Worcestershire sauce

Cut the ends off the courgettes and cut into
rounds. Cook in a saucepan of boiling salted
water for 10 minutes. Drain and arrange the
rounds in the base of a large serving dish or
individual serving dishes. Season with pepper.
Remove the seeds and membranes from the
pepper and cut into thin slices. Slice the
cucumber thinly. Arrange the pepper and
cucumber on top of the courgettes. Sprinkle with
chopped parsley.
Dissolve the gelatine in 2 tablespoons boiling
water. Put in a bowl with the tomato juice and
Worcestershire sauce, mix well.
Pour the tomato sauce mixture over the
vegetables and put in a cool place. Chill
until set.

SAUCES

The fat person can only get slim by re-educating his or her palate and by finding new flavours to replace the old bad habits. That is where these Weight Watchers sauces can be a great help. You will find that they make food even more tasty and exciting than before. Experiment, too. Try your own variations and additions. There are all sorts of extracts, essences and herbs which you are permitted to use. Make good use of flavourings such as Worcestershire sauce, soy sauce, horse-radish and mustard, and learn to enjoy food in its widest sense. Even the simplest dish can be lifted to the heights of superb creation with a good sauce.

Save time by making some of the basic sauces in bulk and store them in the refrigerator so that they are ready for instant use.

MINT SAUCE

Serves Four

2 tablespoons chopped mint
2 tablespoons cider vinegar
2 tablespoons lemon juice
½ teaspoon artificial liquid sweetener

Combine all ingredients in a small bowl.
Leave to stand for 1 hour.

FLAMENCO SAUCE

Serves One

1–3 cloves garlic, crushed
1 tablespoon dried onion flakes
4 fl. oz. tomato juice
2 sticks celery
1 red pepper
2 oz. mushrooms
salt and freshly ground black pepper

Place the garlic, onion flakes and tomato juice in
a saucepan. Bring to the boil and simmer for
10 minutes.
Chop the celery. Remove membranes and seeds
from the pepper and slice thinly. Wash the
mushrooms and cut in quarters. Add all the
prepared vegetables to the saucepan with the salt
and pepper. Cook for a further 10 minutes or
until the vegetables are cooked but still crisp.
Serve the sauce with grilled steak.

Flamenco Sauce with Grilled Steak (p. 18 and 19)

CURRY SAUCE

Serves Four

1 green pepper, deseeded
4 sticks celery
2 tablespoons dried onion flakes
12 fl. oz. tomato juice
2 chicken stock cubes
salt and pepper to taste
1 small can pimentoes
1–2 teaspoons curry powder
few drops artificial liquid sweetener

Slice the pepper and celery. Place them in a
saucepan, with the onion flakes, tomato juice,
stock cubes and salt and pepper and simmer
gently until tender. Chop the pimentoes and add
to the pan with the curry powder and sweetener.
Stir well. Leave to cool and press the mixture
through a sieve or blend at high speed in an
electric blender. Store in screw-top jars in the
refrigerator.

GARLIC AND TARRAGON DRESSING

Serves Eight

8 tablespoons mayonnaise
1 tablespoon tarragon vinegar
1 tablespoon lemon juice
2 tablespoons chopped chives
2 tablespoons chopped parsley
2 cloves garlic, crushed
salt and freshly ground black pepper to taste
4 drops artificial liquid sweetener

Combine all ingredients in a small bowl and
whisk thoroughly. Store in a screw-top jar in
the refrigerator.
Use as required.

WEIGHT WATCHERS BREAD SAUCE

Serves Four

½ pint skimmed milk
large pinch ground cloves
¼ teaspoon salt
freshly ground pepper
1 teaspoon dried onion flakes
4 oz. fresh white breadcrumbs

Place the milk in a saucepan with the ground
cloves, salt, pepper and onion flakes. Bring to
the boil and simmer until the onion is softened.
Stir in the breadcrumbs and combine thoroughly.
Simmer a further 3–4 minutes.
Serve with chicken or turkey.

WEIGHT WATCHERS MAYONNAISE

Serves One

1 tablespoon skimmed milk powder
1 tablespoon cider vinegar
¾ teaspoon dry mustard
artificial sweetener to equal 4 teaspoons sugar
salt and pepper to taste

Place all the ingredients in a bowl and mix
together until thoroughly blended.

WEIGHT WATCHERS STUFFING

Serves Four

4 oz. fresh white breadcrumbs
1 small green pepper
3 sticks celery
1 tablespoon dried thyme
1 teaspoon finely grated lemon rind
2 tablespoons dried onion flakes
salt and pepper
skimmed milk

Prepare the breadcrumbs. Remove the seeds
and membranes from the pepper and chop
finely. Chop the celery finely. Place the
breadcrumbs in a bowl with the pepper, celery,
thyme, lemon rind, onion flakes, salt and
pepper and enough skimmed milk to bind the
mixture together lightly.
Use for stuffing fish or chicken.

EGG AND LEMON SAUCE   Lunch

Serves Two

2 eggs
3 tablespoons lemon juice
3 tablespoons beef or chicken stock made with stock
    cube and water
salt and pepper

Put the eggs into a bowl and whisk them well
until thickened. Whisk in the lemon juice
gradually, then the stock.
Pour the sauce into a saucepan and heat very
gently, stirring constantly, until thickened.
Season to taste. Serve with fish.

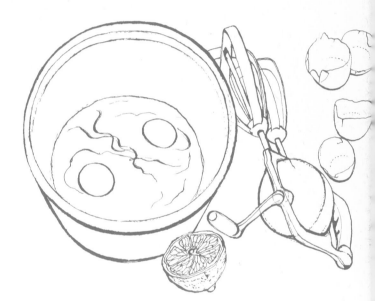

COTTAGE CHEESE DIP   Lunch

Serves Two

4 oz. cottage cheese
2 eggs, separated
1 teaspoon lemon juice
½ teaspoon French mustard
salt and pepper
2 slices of toast

Sieve the cottage cheese and remove all the
lumps. Put it in a bowl and beat in the egg
yolks, lemon juice, French mustard, salt and
pepper. Whisk the egg whites until stiff and fold
into the cottage cheese mixture.
Serve with fingers of toast.

FLUFFY SALAD SAUCE

Serves Two

2 eggs
artificial sweetener to taste
pinch of salt
pinch of pepper
½ teaspoon dry mustard
1 tablespoon vinegar
2 tablespoons vegetable oil

Cook 1 egg until hard boiled. Shell and remove the yolk. Separate the uncooked egg and place the raw egg yolk with the cooked yolk in a bowl. Beat the yolks together with a wooden spoon. Add the seasonings, vinegar and oil. Beat very well until combined and thickened. Chop the cooked egg white finely and stir into the sauce. Whisk the raw egg white until stiff and carefully fold into the sauce.
Serve with fish and salad.

TOMATO SAUCE

For fish, meat, poultry, spaghetti, etc.

1½ pints tomato juice
2 tablespoons dried pepper flakes
1 tablespoon dried onion flakes
4 tablespoons cider vinegar
2 teaspoons Worcestershire sauce
½ teaspoon artificial liquid sweetener
¼ teaspoon celery salt
¼ teaspoon pepper
½ teaspoon Aromat
1 teaspoon salt
½ teaspoon dried tarragon

Combine all the ingredients in a saucepan. Bring to the boil, stirring occasionally and cook rapidly until reduced by one third. Allow to cool completely, pour into an electric blender and blend at high speed until smooth. Store in screw-top jars in the refrigerator. Use as desired.
Note: This sauce is also good when used before blending.

Weight Watchers Bread Sauce (opposite)

PRAWN COCKTAIL SAUCE

Serves Eight

8 fl. oz. tomato juice
½ teaspoon grated horse-radish
1 teaspoon Worcestershire sauce
2 teaspoons lemon juice
½ teaspoon garlic powder
8 tablespoons mayonnaise
salt and pepper

Place the tomato juice in a small saucepan.
Bring to the boil and boil briskly until reduced
to half the quantity. Cool. Stir in all other
ingredients and chill.
Serve with shell fish.

ONION SAUCE

Serves One

4 oz. onion
4 fl. oz. water
salt and pepper to taste
1 slice bread, crumbed
2 tablespoons skimmed milk powder

Chop the onion finely and place it in a small
saucepan with the water and seasonings.
Simmer gently until tender. Stir in breadcrumbs
and cook for 2–3 minutes. Cool slightly then
whisk in the milk powder.

ASPARAGUS SAUCE

Serves Two

1 × 15 oz. can asparagus
1 oz. skimmed milk powder
salt and pepper to taste

Do not drain the asparagus. Place all the
ingredients in an electric blender and blend until
smooth and creamy. Heat slowly.
Serve with fish, chicken, rabbit or veal.

HORSE-RADISH TARRAGON SAUCE

Serves Six—Makes about ¾ pint

2 teaspoons grated fresh horse-radish
1 tablespoon tarragon vinegar
3 tablespoons lemon juice
¼ pint water
artificial sweetener to equal 1 tablespoon sugar
1 teaspoon salt
1 teaspoon paprika pepper
6 oz. skimmed milk powder

Place all the ingredients in an electric blender.
Turn on to the highest speed for 30 seconds or
until the sauce is well blended. Chill for 2 hours
before using.

MINT JELLY

Serves Four

6 tablespoons wine vinegar
scant ½ oz. gelatine
10–15 drops artificial liquid sweetener (according to
    taste)
few drops green food colouring
2–3 tablespoons chopped fresh mint

Put the wine vinegar into a measuring jug and
stir in the gelatine. Pour in enough boiling water
to make ¾ pint liquid. Stir to dissolve the
gelatine. Stir in the artificial sweetener, food
colouring and mint.
Allow to cool then pour into a screw-top jar
and put in a cool place to set.

EGGS AND CHEESES

As you will see in this chapter, eggs and cheese are very versatile foods which are the base for all sorts of exciting dishes. Here you will find recipes for both breakfast and lunch, equally important meals if you are slimming the Weight Watchers way. Try out a new recipe every few days and make food fun. With an attractive meal in front of you to whet your appetite, you will find it much easier to dismiss any thoughts you may have for undesirable, fattening foods. Like other recipes in this book, many of these are prize-winning ones submitted by British Weight Watchers. They created them at home in their own kitchens, using their ingenuity and imagination to provide delicious alternatives to the bad old recipes which used to make them fat.

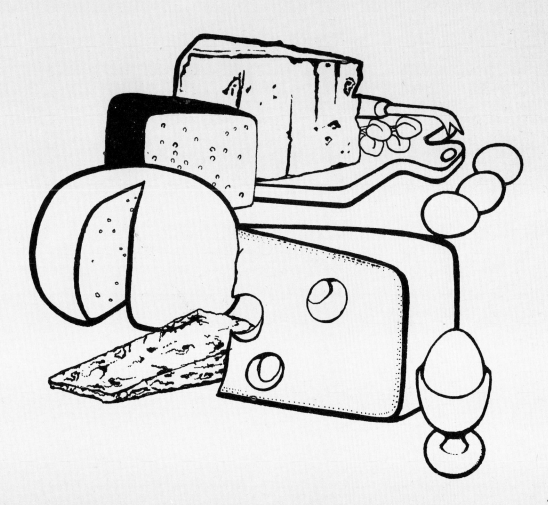

APPLE MEDLEY Breakfast

Serves Two

2 red-skinned apples
2 tablespoons low calorie squash
½ pint water
2 slices white or brown bread
4 oz. cottage cheese
¼ teaspoon ground cinnamon

Core and slice the apples. Place in an oven-proof dish with the squash and water. Cook in the centre of a moderate oven (350°F. Mark 4) for 15–20 minutes until tender.
Toast the bread on one side only. Spread the cheese on the untoasted side of the bread and arrange the cooked apple on top. Sprinkle with cinnamon and baste with a little of the liquid in the dish. Brown the top lightly under a hot grill.

ASPARAGUS CHEESE Lunch

Serves One

3 spears asparagus
1 slice toast
2 oz. Cheddar cheese
salt

Cook the asparagus in boiling salted water until tender. Drain well. Arrange the spears on the slice of toast. Sprinkle the grated cheese over the top. Cook under a hot grill until the cheese has melted and browned lightly.
Serve as soon as possible.

BAKED MUSHROOM PIE Lunch

Serves Four

8 oz. mushrooms
1 teaspoon dried onion flakes
scant ¼ pint chicken stock made with chicken stock cube and water
4 oz. fresh white breadcrumbs
2 tablespoons tomato juice
4 oz. cooked chicken
salt and pepper
4 eggs
4 fl. oz. skimmed milk
1 tablespoon chopped parsley
2 oz. grated Cheddar cheese

Chop the mushrooms, place in a saucepan with the onion flakes and a little stock. Cook,

stirring, 2–3 minutes. Add the breadcrumbs, tomato juice, chicken and remaining stock. Season to taste. Pour into a shallow ovenproof dish.
Beat the eggs lightly with the milk and parsley. Pour over the chicken mixture and sprinkle the top with grated cheese. Place the dish in a pan containing ½ inch cold water. Bake in a moderate oven (350°F. Mark 4) for approximately 30 minutes.

CAULIFLOWER AND EGGS Lunch

Serves One

½ small cauliflower
2 eggs
½ teaspoon caraway seeds (optional)
salt and pepper
1 slice toast

Wash the cauliflower and divide into flowerettes. Cook in a saucepan of boiling salted water for about 15 minutes or until just tender. Drain.
Beat the eggs in a bowl with the caraway seeds, salt and pepper. Put the cauliflower in a saucepan, add the eggs and cook, gently, stirring continuously until the eggs are set. Place the toast on a serving plate and top with the cauliflower mixture. Brown the top under a grill if liked.

CAULIFLOWER AND EGG PUFF Lunch

Serves Two

1 small cauliflower
2 slices bread
2 oz. grated Cheddar cheese
2 eggs, separated
salt and pepper to taste

Break the cauliflower into flowerettes and cook in boiling salted water for 10–12 minutes. Drain well.
Toast the bread on both sides and cut into small triangles.
Place the cauliflower in an ovenproof dish, sprinkle with half of the cheese. Whisk the egg whites until stiff and spoon over the cauliflower, leaving two hollows in the middle. Carefully place an egg yolk in each hollow and season with salt and pepper. Sprinkle the remaining cheese on the top and cook under a hot grill until the yolks are set.
Serve garnished with the toast triangles.

CAULIFLOWER BREAD Lunch

Serves Two

1 cauliflower
¼ pint skimmed milk
pinch of ground cloves
2 oz. breadcrumbs
salt and pepper
4 eggs
4 tablespoons tomato juice
2 tablespoons chopped parsley
paprika pepper

Break the cauliflower into flowerettes and cook in boiling salted water until tender. Drain well. Press the cooked cauliflower through a sieve. Place in a bowl and stir in the skimmed milk, cloves, breadcrumbs, salt and pepper.
Beat 2 eggs with 2 egg yolks and add to the cauliflower mixture with the tomato juice. Mix well. Whisk the remaining 2 egg whites until stiff and fold into the cauliflower mixture. Carefully pour the mixture into a mould. Stand the mould in another pan with water to come half way up the sides. Bake in a moderate oven (350°F. Mark 4) for about 45 minutes.
Serve sprinkled with chopped parsley and paprika pepper. It is a good accompaniment for asparagus tips.

CAULIFLOWER AND MUSHROOM SAVOURY Lunch

Serves One

½ clove garlic, crushed
½ pint skimmed milk
8 oz. mushrooms
salt and pepper
2 teaspoons chopped parsley
1 small cauliflower
2 oz. grated Cheddar cheese
1 slice toast

Put the garlic and milk together in a saucepan. Chop the mushrooms, add to the pan with the salt, pepper and parsley. Bring to the boil, cover pan and simmer for about 20 minutes. Meanwhile, break the cauliflower into flowerettes and cook in a saucepan with boiling salted water to cover, until tender. Drain. Place the cooked cauliflower in an ovenproof serving dish, pour the mushroom mixture over and sprinkle with the cheese. Cook under a hot grill until the cheese has melted and is beginning to brown.
Serve hot with a slice of toast.

Apple Medley (below)

CELERY WITH CHEESE

Serves Two

2 oz. celery sticks
2 oz. grated Cheddar cheese
2 oz. breadcrumbs
salt and pepper
green pepper for garnish

Place the celery, cut into neat lengths, in an
ovenproof dish. Cover with boiling water.
Cover the dish with foil and cook in a moderate
oven (350°F. Mark 4) until the celery is tender.
Drain off the liquid.
Mix the cheese with the breadcrumbs in a bowl
and season well. Sprinkle the cheese mixture
over the celery and return to the oven until the
top is beginning to brown.
Serve the celery garnished with thinly sliced
rings of green pepper.

CHEESE SANDWICH SOUFFLÉ

Serves One

1 slice bread
prepared mustard
1 oz. grated cheese
1 egg
¼ pint skimmed milk
salt and pepper to taste
cooked cauliflower for serving

Cut the bread in half and sandwich together
with a little prepared mustard and the cheese.
Place in a shallow ovenproof dish. Beat the
egg with the milk, season to taste and pour over
the sandwich. Cover the dish with foil and bake
in a moderate oven (350°F. Mark 4) for about
30 minutes.
Serve with cooked cauliflower.

CHEESE EGG

Serves Two

1 egg
1 tablespoon skimmed milk
½ teaspoon dry mustard
salt and pepper
1 oz. grated Cheddar cheese
2 slices toast

Either hard boil or poach the egg. Place it in a
small ovenproof dish.
Mix the skimmed milk with the mustard, salt,
pepper and cheese together in a small saucepan.
Heat gently, stirring continuously, until the
cheese is melted.
Spoon the sauce over the egg then cook under a
hot grill until the top is golden.
Serve with fingers of toast.

CHEESE STUFFED MARROW

Serves Four

1 marrow
1 lb. cottage cheese
2 teaspoons chopped chives
2 inches cucumber
salt and pepper
½ pint tomato juice

Cut the marrow in half lengthwise and
carefully scoop out the seeds. Place the
hollowed halves in an ovenproof dish.
Place the cottage cheese in a bowl and mix with
the chives. Peel and chop the cucumber finely
and stir into the cheese with salt and pepper to
taste.
Fill the marrow halves with the cheese mixture
then sandwich the two halves, cut sides
together. Tie with fine string in two or three
places. Pour the tomato juice over the marrow
and cover with foil. Cook in a moderate oven
(350°F. Mark 4) for 30–40 minutes or until the
marrow is tender.

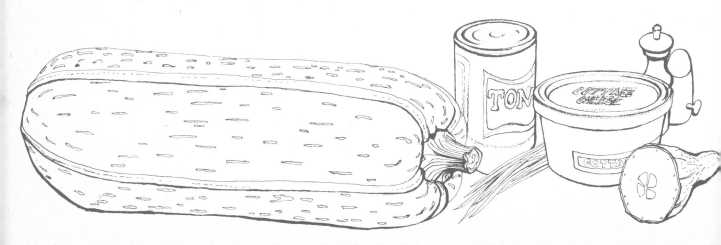

COTTAGE CHEESE SALAD   Lunch

Serves One

¼ small red cabbage
2 sticks celery
1 red-skinned apple
3 inches cucumber
4 oz. cottage cheese
1 teaspoon lemon juice

Dressing:
salt and pepper
1 teaspoon German mustard
1 tablespoon vinegar
2 tablespoons skimmed milk
1 tablespoon vegetable oil

Shred the cabbage finely. Chop the celery. Chop the washed, unpeeled apple. Cut the unpeeled cucumber into dice. Mix all the prepared vegetables in a bowl.
Place all the dressing ingredients in a small bowl and whisk with a fork until well blended. Pour over the vegetables and toss lightly.
Mix the cottage cheese with the lemon juice. Arrange the salad on a serving dish and pile the cottage cheese on top.

COURGETTE AND MUSHROOM SAVOURY   Lunch

Serves Two

6–8 courgettes (according to size)
3 tablespoons chicken stock made with chicken stock
　　cube and water
4 oz. mushrooms
lemon juice to taste
salt and pepper
4 oz. grated Cheddar cheese
2 slices bread, toasted

Top and tail the courgettes. Place them in a saucepan of boiling water and cook for 2 minutes. (This eliminates any bitter taste). Drain and rinse under cold water. Cut into ¾ inch slices.
Heat a non-stick frying pan, add the courgettes and chicken stock, cover and simmer for about 15 minutes or until almost tender. Slice the mushrooms and add to the pan with the lemon juice and seasonings. Cook, covered, for a further 5 minutes. Uncover the pan, increase the heat and boil briskly until the liquid is reduced. Divide the mixture between two heatproof serving dishes. Sprinkle 2 oz. cheese over each dish and cook under a hot grill until browned. Serve as soon as possible, accompanied by toast.

BELGIAN SPINACH   Lunch

Serves One

¾ lb. spinach
grated nutmeg
salt and pepper
2 eggs, beaten

Wash the spinach, cook in a covered saucepan with a very little water, until tender. Drain well. Stir in nutmeg, salt and pepper to taste. Stir in the beaten egg just before serving.

DEVILLED BUCK   Lunch

Serves One

1 slice bread
1 oz. Cheddar cheese
½ dessert apple
curry powder
1 egg
cooked sliced green beans

Toast the bread. Slice the cheese thinly, peel, core and slice the apple. Arrange the cheese slices on the toast and top with the apple. Sprinkle with curry powder to taste. Place under a moderately slow grill and cook until the apple is tender and the cheese is beginning to melt. Meanwhile, poach the egg and cook the beans. Place the toast on a serving plate, top with the poached egg and serve with green beans.

EGG AND CHEESE SALAD   Lunch

Serves One

1 hard boiled egg
pinch of salt
pinch of pepper
pinch of onion powder
2 oz. cottage cheese or 1 oz. grated Cheshire cheese
1 teaspoon finely chopped green pepper
1 tablespoon mayonnaise
lettuce
white cabbage

Shell and chop the egg and sprinkle it with the seasonings. Mix the cheese with the green pepper and mayonnaise, then combine lightly with the egg.
Arrange some lettuce and shredded cabbage on a serving plate, top with the egg and cheese mixture.

ENGLISH CHEESE CAKES   Breakfast

Serves Two

2 oz. white fresh breadcrumbs
1 egg, beaten
1 oz. grated Cheddar cheese
salt and pepper to taste
2 teaspoons dried onion flakes
skimmed milk if necessary
cucumber for garnish

Mix together in a bowl the breadcrumbs, egg, cheese, salt, pepper and onion flakes. Mix thoroughly, adding a little skimmed milk if necessary to make a thick paste.
Shape the mixture into round cakes, approximately $\frac{1}{4}$ inch thick. Heat a non-stick frying pan and cook the cheese cakes for 5 minutes, turning frequently.
Serve the cheese cakes garnished with thin slices of cucumber.

EGGS IN THICK CURRY SAUCE   Lunch

Serves One

2 teaspoons curry powder
salt and pepper to taste
artificial liquid sweetener to equal 2 teaspoons
    sugar
8 oz. cooked, drained marrow
4 oz. button mushrooms
1 large stick celery
2 hard-boiled eggs
$\frac{1}{4}$ red pepper
$\frac{1}{4}$ green pepper
3 oz. cooked rice
chopped parsley for garnish

Put the curry powder in a saucepan with $\frac{1}{4}$ pint water, salt, pepper and artificial sweetener. Bring to the boil, add the marrow and mash well. Simmer for 5 minutes. Slice the mushrooms, chop the celery and add them to the saucepan. Cover and simmer for a further 10 minutes. Cut the eggs in half lengthwise, cut the peppers into matchstick strips, add to the pan and reheat.
Arrange the hot, freshly cooked rice on a serving plate and spoon the eggs and curry sauce on top. Serve garnished with chopped parsley.

EGG FLORENTINE   Lunch

Serves One

small packet of frozen spinach
1 egg
1 oz. grated Cheddar cheese

Cook the spinach in boiling salted water, drain well. Poach the egg.
Arrange the spinach in a small heatproof dish, place the egg on the spinach. Sprinkle the grated cheese over the egg and place under a hot grill. Cook until the cheese is melted and golden.

EGG BOAT   Lunch

Serves One

1 oz. fresh white breadcrumbs
1 oz. grated Cheddar cheese
large pinch of mustard
few drops Worcestershire sauce
salt and pepper
2 tablespoons skimmed milk
1 egg, separated
1 teaspoon tomato juice
cayenne pepper
small packet of frozen spinach

Place the breadcrumbs in a bowl with the cheese, mustard, Worcestershire sauce, salt, pepper and skimmed milk. Combine thoroughly then form the mixture into a flat 'cake' and place on a piece of foil or a baking tray.
Whisk the egg white until stiff and spread it over the cheese mixture, making a hollow in the centre. Carefully put the egg yolk in the hollow. Spoon the tomato juice over the yolk and sprinkle all over with salt and cayenne pepper. Bake in a hot oven (400°F. Mark 6) for 20–25 minutes until the yolk is set and the white is golden brown and crisp.
Meanwhile cook the spinach and arrange it on a serving plate. Place the egg boat on top.

Egg Florentine (opposite)

FLUFFY MUSHROOM OMELETTE

Breakfast

Serves Two

2 oz. mushrooms
2 eggs, separated
2 tablespoons skimmed milk
salt and pepper
2 slices toast

Wash the mushrooms and chop.
Whisk the egg whites until stiff, stir in the egg yolks, milk, salt and pepper.
Heat a non-stick frying pan and cook the mushrooms for 2–3 minutes, stirring constantly. Add the egg mixture and cook until the underneath is golden. Place the frying pan under a hot grill and cook until the top is browned.
Serve immediately, with toast.

EGGS WITH CURRIED VEGETABLES

Lunch

Serves One

2 oz. red or green pepper
1 dessert apple
1 teaspoon dried onion flakes
salt and pepper to taste
1–3 teaspoons curry powder
¼ pint tomato juice or water
2 oz. mushrooms
3 oz. cooked rice
2 hard-boiled eggs

Chop the pepper finely, peel, core and slice the apple thinly. Place pepper and apple in a saucepan with the onion flakes, salt and pepper, curry powder to taste and tomato juice. Bring to the boil, cover the pan and simmer for 10 minutes or until the pepper is tender.
Wash the mushrooms, chop them and add to the saucepan. Cook a further 10 minutes.
Arrange the hot freshly cooked rice on a serving plate, top with the hot freshly boiled eggs, cut in slices. Coat the eggs with the curried vegetables. Serve immediately.

GOLDEN COATED CAULIFLOWER

Lunch

Serves One

½ small cauliflower
1 tablespoon skimmed milk
½ teaspoon made mustard
salt and pepper
2 oz. grated Cheddar cheese
1 tablespoon mayonnaise
1 oz. white breadcrumbs
green salad for serving

Cook the cauliflower in boiling salted water until just tender. Drain thoroughly and place in a shallow heatproof dish.
Put the milk, mustard, salt, pepper and cheese in a saucepan. Heat gently, stirring, until the cheese has melted and the mixture is smooth. Stir in the mayonnaise. Spoon the sauce over the cooked cauliflower and sprinkle the breadcrumbs on top. Place under a moderately hot grill until the top is golden.
Serve a green salad separately.

FRENCH CHEESE SOUFFLÉ

Lunch

Serves Two

¼ pint skimmed milk
2 oz. fresh white breadcrumbs
2 oz. grated Cheddar cheese
salt and pepper to taste
pinch of cayenne pepper
pinch of dry mustard
2 eggs, separated

Heat the milk very gently in a saucepan. Add the breadcrumbs, cheese, seasonings and egg yolks. Whisk the egg whites until stiff and gently fold them into the cheese mixture. Pour gently into a 6 inch diameter soufflé dish and bake in a hot oven (425°F. Mark 7) for about 15 minutes or until well-risen and cooked.

LASAGNE   Lunch

Serves Two

1 lb. courgettes
½ pint tomato juice
1 chicken stock cube
2 tablespoons dried onion flakes
salt, pepper and Tabasco sauce to taste
6 oz. cooked noodles or lasagne
3 oz. grated Cheddar cheese
1 oz. grated Parmesan cheese

Slice the courgettes. Place the tomato juice in a
large non-stick frying pan with the chicken
stock cube. Heat gently, stirring, until the stock
cube is dissolved. Add the courgettes, onion
flakes and seasonings. Bring to the boil and cook
rapidly until the liquid has almost evaporated,
about 10–15 minutes.
Place a layer of the courgettes in the base of a
heatproof dish. Add a layer of hot freshly
cooked noodles, cover with more courgettes,
then the remaining noodles and the remaining
courgettes. Sprinkle the top with the grated
cheeses and place under a hot grill until the
cheese has melted.

LIPTAUER CHEESE   Lunch

Serves Two

1 teaspoon dried onion flakes
8 oz. cottage cheese
1 teaspoon paprika pepper
2 teaspoons chopped gherkins
1 teaspoon chopped capers
2 teaspoons chopped chives
salt and pepper to taste
¼ teaspoon Worcestershire sauce

Soak the onion flakes until reconstituted.
Mix all the ingredients together in a bowl and
beat very well until thoroughly combined and
creamy.
Serve with a salad or spread on celery sticks.

MARROW AU GRATIN   Lunch

Serves One

8 oz. marrow
salt
2 oz. Cheddar cheese
paprika pepper

Peel the marrow, remove the pips and cut into
cubes. Cook in a covered saucepan with ½ inch
boiling water until tender. Drain well.
Place the cooked marrow in a shallow ovenproof dish. Cut the cheese into thin slices and
place it on top of the marrow.
Sprinkle with paprika pepper and cook under a
moderate grill until the cheese is melted and
golden.

MOCK PIZZA   Lunch

Serves Two

1 green pepper
2 red peppers
¼ pint tomato juice
2 oz. fresh white breadcrumbs
2 eggs
2 oz. grated Cheddar cheese
½ teaspoon mixed dried herbs
salt and pepper

Remove the membranes and seeds from the
peppers. Slice the green pepper into rings and
cook in boiling water for 5 minutes. Rinse in
cold water and drain well. Chop the red
peppers and put into a saucepan with the
tomato juice. Bring to the boil then simmer,
uncovered, until the pepper is very tender.
Mash well.
Place the breadcrumbs in a non-stick frying pan
and cook gently until beginning to brown.
Beat the eggs with half of the cheese, herbs, salt
and pepper. Pour the eggs into the pan, mix
with the crumbs and cook until golden
underneath. Brown the top under a hot grill.
Invert the pan over a heatproof serving plate
to transfer the pizza base. Spread the base with
the mashed red pepper, arrange the green pepper
rings on top and sprinkle with the remaining
cheese. Place under a hot grill until the top of
the pizza is golden brown.
Serve as soon as possible.

French Cheese Soufflé (p. 34)

MUSHROOM CHEESE ON TOAST
Breakfast

Serves Two

4 oz. button mushrooms
skimmed milk
2 slices bread
2 oz. hard cheese

Wash the mushrooms and slice thinly. Place the mushrooms in a non-stick frying pan with enough skimmed milk to almost cover. Simmer gently until the mushrooms are tender. Drain well.
Toast the slices of bread on both sides, pile the mushrooms on top and grate the cheese over the mushrooms. Place under a hot grill until the cheese is golden.

MUSHROOMS BAKED WITH CHEESE STUFFING
Lunch

Serves One

4 large fresh mushrooms
2 oz. Cheddar cheese
1 slice bread, toasted
2 tablespoons chopped parsley
large pinch onion powder
large pinch garlic powder
salt and freshly ground black pepper
rind $\frac{1}{4}$ lemon
1 teaspoon lemon juice
watercress for garnish

Wipe the mushrooms with a damp cloth.
Remove the stalks and place these in an electric blender with the cheese, bread, parsley, and seasonings. Blend at the highest speed until the mixture is smooth.
Fill the mushroom caps with this mixture. Place in an ovenproof dish and bake in a moderately slow oven (325°F. Mark 3) for 15–20 minutes.
Serve garnished with sprigs of watercress.

Mushrooms Baked with Cheese Stuffing (top p. 35)

Mock Pizza (bottom p. 35)

PIPERADE
Lunch

Serves Two

3 large green or red peppers
2 tablespoons dried onion flakes
1 clove garlic, crushed
salt and freshly ground black pepper
$\frac{1}{2}$ teaspoon dried basil
6 fl. oz. tomato juice
4 eggs, beaten
2 slices toast

Grill the peppers all over under a hot grill until the skin is blackened. Wash the skin off. Cut the peppers into thin strips, removing the seeds and membranes. Place the prepared peppers in a small saucepan with the onion flakes, garlic, salt and pepper, basil and tomato juice. Bring to the boil and simmer, uncovered, for about 10 minutes or until soft and very tender.
Add the beaten eggs and continue cooking, very gently, stirring continuously, until the mixture is creamy and the eggs are set.
Serve with fingers of toast.

PEACH AND COTTAGE CHEESE SALAD
Breakfast

Serves Two

2 fresh peaches
lemon juice
4 oz. cottage cheese
lettuce
$\frac{1}{3}$ cucumber
canned peppers for garnish
2 slices toasted bread for serving
2 tablespoons mayonnaise for serving

Peel, halve and stone the peaches, sprinkle the cut surfaces with lemon juice. Fill the cavities with cottage cheese.
Arrange a bed of crisp lettuce leaves on a serving plate. Grate the cucumber and arrange it on the lettuce. Sprinkle with lemon juice. Place the stuffed peaches on the cucumber and garnish with strips of canned pepper.
Serve with the slices of toasted bread and the mayonnaise.

POTATO PANCAKES   Lunch

Serves One

3 oz. cooked potato
1 slice bread
2 eggs, beaten
pinch of salt
$\frac{1}{4}$ teaspoon dried onion flakes
1 tablespoon skimmed milk

Mash the potato. Make the bread into bread-crumbs and beat with the potato, eggs, salt, onion flakes and skimmed milk.
Heat a non-stick frying pan and drop tablespoons of the mixture into the pan. Cook until browned on both sides, turning once.

SAVOURY EGG CUSTARD WITH
TOMATO SAUCE   Lunch

Serves One

2 eggs
pinch of grated nutmeg
salt and pepper
$\frac{1}{2}$ pint skimmed milk

Tomato Sauce:
$\frac{1}{2}$ oz. skimmed milk powder
$\frac{1}{2}$ pint tomato juice
$\frac{1}{4}$ teaspoon garlic powder, to taste
$\frac{1}{4}$ teaspoon dried marjoram
artificial sweetener to taste
salt and pepper

Place the eggs in a bowl and mix gently with a fork. Stir in the nutmeg, salt and pepper. Heat the milk in a small saucepan until warm, pour on to the eggs, stirring just until all the ingredients are mixed. Pour into an ovenproof serving dish. Stand the dish in a roasting pan with enough water to come halfway up the sides of the dish. Bake in a slow oven (300°F. Mark 2) for about $1\frac{1}{4}$ hours or until custard is set.
Meanwhile, place all the ingredients for the sauce in an electric blender and blend for 30 seconds. Alternatively, place the ingredients in a bowl and whisk until thoroughly combined. Pour into a saucepan, bring to the boil and simmer for 10–15 minutes.
Serve the egg custard and the sauce separately.

SAVOURY BAKED APPLES   Lunch

Serves Two

2 medium cooking apples
4 oz. cottage cheese
2 oz. grated Cheddar cheese
$\frac{1}{4}$ teaspoon dry mustard
salt and pepper to taste
lettuce for serving
chopped mushrooms and celery for garnish

Cut the apples in half and scoop out the centre, leaving a shell about $\frac{1}{4}$ inch thick. Remove the core and chop the remainder. Mix the apple with the cottage cheese, Cheddar cheese, mustard, salt and pepper. Refill the halves with the cheese mixture, put the halves together to make whole apples again and wrap in foil. Place them on a baking tray and cook in a moderately hot oven (375°F. Mark 5) for 1–$1\frac{1}{4}$ hours or until very tender.
Arrange a bed of lettuce on a serving plate, place the cooked apples on top and garnish with raw mushrooms and celery.

PORTUGUESE EGGS   Lunch

Serves Two

2 green peppers
2 tablespoons dried onion flakes
12 fl. oz. tomato juice
$\frac{1}{2}$ chicken stock cube
2 eggs
2 oz. grated Cheddar cheese
2 slices toast

Remove the seeds and membranes from the peppers and slice thinly. Put them in a saucepan with the onion flakes, tomato juice and the stock cube. Bring to the boil, stirring, cover and simmer until the peppers are tender. Add a little water if necessary.
Spoon the mixture into an ovenproof serving dish, make two hollows and carefully break an egg into each one. Cook in a hot oven (400°F. Mark 6) for 10–15 minutes. Three minutes before the cooking time is finished, sprinkle with cheese.
Serve as soon as possible, with the toast.

Savoury Egg Custard with Tomato Sauce (top p. 38)
Portuguese Eggs (bottom p. 38)

Spanish Omelette (top p. 39)

Tomato White Cap Aspic (bottom p. 39)

SAVOURY EGGS   Lunch

Serves Two

4 eggs
½ teaspoon curry powder
salt and pepper
2 oz. brown breadcrumbs

Hard boil 2 eggs, cool, remove the shells and
slice into thick rounds. Arrange the slices of
egg in an ovenproof dish, sprinkle them with
the curry powder.
Beat the remaining 2 eggs and season well.
Pour them over the hard-boiled eggs and cover
the dish with the breadcrumbs. Bake in a
moderate oven (350°F. Mark 4) for 15–20
minutes. Serve hot.

SPANISH OMELETTE   Breakfast

Serves Two

2 eggs
salt and pepper
1 tablespoon chopped green pepper
1 tablespoon chopped red pepper
1 tablespoon chopped mushrooms
1 tablespoon dried onion flakes, soaked
2 slices toast

Beat the eggs with the salt and pepper and one
tablespoon water.
Cook the chopped peppers in a saucepan of
boiling water for 1 minute. Rinse in cold water.
Heat a non-stick frying pan gently. Add the
eggs and cook until beginning to set. Sprinkle
all the prepared vegetables on top and cook
gently for 1 minute. Place the omelette under a
hot grill to cook top. Serve without folding,
with toast.

SPINACH SAVOURY   Lunch

Serves One

1 small packet frozen spinach
salt
1 oz. grated cheese
1 egg
1 oz. breadcrumbs
1 oz. skimmed milk powder
3 tablespoons water
onion salt and pepper to taste

Cook the spinach in boiling salted water until
tender. Drain very well.
Place a layer of grated cheese in the base of a
small ovenproof dish. Cover with a layer of
cooked spinach, then a layer of cheese, another
of spinach and a final layer of cheese. Beat the
egg and pour over all. Put the breadcrumbs in a
bowl and mix in the milk powder, water,
onion, salt and pepper. Spread over the top of
the layered spinach and cheese.
Cook in a hot oven (400°F. Mark 6) for
30–35 minutes.

STUFFED EGGS   Lunch

Serves One

2 hard-boiled eggs
½ teaspoon snipped chives
pinch of chervil
salt and pepper
1 tablespoon mayonnaise
green salad for serving

Cook the eggs, rinse in cold water and shell.
Cut each egg in half and carefully remove the
yolk. Put the yolks in a bowl with the chives,
chervil, salt and pepper. Mash with a fork and
add enough mayonnaise to make a soft paste.
Place the egg whites on a serving plate and pile
the yolk mixture back into the hollows.
Serve with a green salad.

TOMATO WHITE CAP ASPIC   Lunch

Serves Two

¾ pint tomato juice
scant ½ oz. gelatine
salt and pepper
1 tablespoon lemon juice
8 oz. cottage cheese
2 tablespoons finely chopped celery
2 tablespoons finely chopped red pepper
1 tablespoon snipped chives
green salad for serving

Pour ¼ pint tomato juice in to a small saucepan, heat gently until almost boiling. Sprinkle in the gelatine and stir until dissolved. Add the cold juice and season with salt and pepper and lemon juice. Pour into a mould or 2 individual moulds and put in a cold place until set.
Mix the cottage cheese with the celery, pepper and chives in a bowl. Season.
Arrange a bed of green salad vegetables on a serving plate, unmould the tomato mould on top. Place the cottage cheese mixture on the jellied tomato. Serve as soon as possible.

STUFFED GREEN PEPPER   Lunch

Serves One

1 medium-sized green pepper
1 slice bread
2 tablespoons skimmed milk
2 oz. grated Cheddar cheese
2 tablespoons tomato juice
1 teaspoon dried onion flakes
pinch of dried mixed herbs
salt and pepper
garlic powder (optional)

Cut the top off the pepper, reserve the top. Carefully scoop out the seeds and membranes from the pepper and wash carefully. Drop the pepper and top into a saucepan of boiling water and cook for about 3 minutes. Remove and drain.
Crumble the bread into a bowl, add the milk to soften it. Mix in the cheese, tomato juice, onion flakes, herbs, salt, pepper and garlic powder with a fork.
Fill the pepper with the stuffing, replace the top and stand it in a shallow ovenproof dish. Pour about ¼ inch water into the base of the dish. Cook in a moderate oven (350°F. Mark 4) for 30–35 minutes or until the pepper is tender. Baste with water occasionally.

SWEDISH CUCUMBER   Lunch

Serves Two

1 small cucumber
4 oz grated Cheddar cheese
1 tablespoon chopped chives
1 teaspoon chopped mint
salt and pepper
4 oz. button mushrooms
radishes and watercress for serving

Wash the cucumber and cut it in half lengthwise. Scoop out the flesh carefully, leaving a thin-walled shell. Grate the cucumber and mix with half of the grated cheese, chives, mint, salt and pepper. Refill the cucumber shells.
Wash the mushrooms, cut off the stalks, level with the caps. Cook in a saucepan of boiling water for 5 minutes. Drain well.
Arrange the mushrooms on the cucumber and sprinkle the remaining cheese over the top. Place under a moderately hot grill until the cheese is melted and golden brown.
Arrange the cucumber on a serving plate with the radishes and watercress.

WEIGHT WATCHERS QUICHE LORRAINE   Lunch

Serves Two

2 slices bread
4 oz. cooked veal or chicken
¼ teaspoon garlic powder
1 teaspoon dried onion flakes
2 eggs
salt and cayenne pepper
pinch of grated nutmeg
8 fl. oz. skimmed milk

Roll the slices of bread with a rolling pin until thin. Cover an ovenproof plate with the slices of bread. Chop the veal or chicken and scatter it over the bread with the garlic powder and onion flakes.
Beat the eggs in a bowl with the salt, cayenne pepper, nutmeg and warm milk. Pour on to the bread and bake in a hot oven (400°F. Mark 6) for 20–25 minutes.

Stuffed Eggs (p. 42)

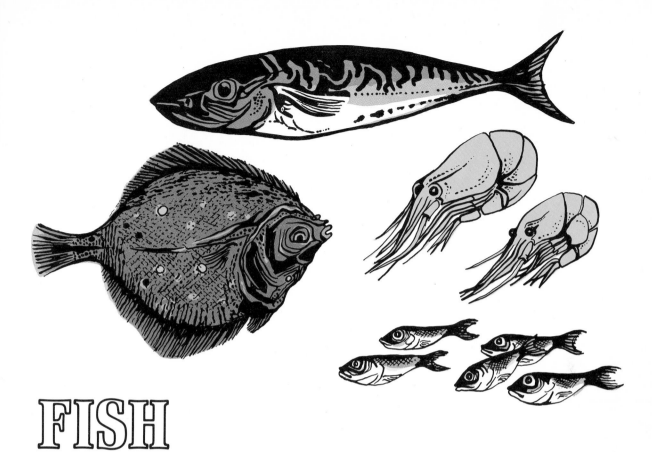

FISH

Fish plays a very important part in the Weight Watchers Programme. To enjoy it at its best buy it the day it is to be eaten and when buying a whole fish watch for shining scales and eyes which are an indication of its freshness. When buying frozen or canned fish, check the net weight of the packet or can. It may be under or over your allowance. Whatever food you buy, always look closely at the labels. "Accidental" cheating is only too easy if you shop carelessly. Remember, all canned fish must be drained of oil before use.

These are the basic methods of cooking fish:

To grill—place whole fish or fillet on foil, sprinkle generously with lemon juice and seasoning. Cook under a hot grill until fish flakes easily.

To poach—place fish in a pan and cover with salted water. Simmer gently until fish flakes easily. Serve with a Weight Watchers sauce.

To steam—put fish on a plate and place on top of a saucepan of boiling water. Sprinkle fish with lemon juice and seasoning, cover with a second plate and cook until fish flakes easily.

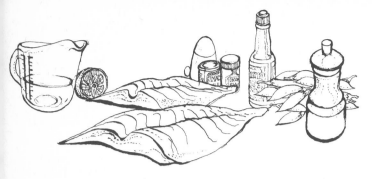

¼ *teaspoon paprika pepper*
chopped parsley for garnish
green salad for serving

Tartare Sauce:
2 tablespoons mayonnaise
1 teaspoon chopped capers
1 teaspoon chopped gherkin
1 teaspoon finely chopped parsley

Cut the cod into large cubes, remove the seeds
and membranes from the pepper and cut into
1 inch pieces. Peel the onions and leave whole.
Quarter the tomatoes and wash the mushrooms.
Place the cod in a saucepan with the pepper and
onions. Cover with water, bring to the boil and
simmer for 5 minutes. Drain.
Thread the cod, vegetables and bay leaves onto
4 skewers. Sprinkle with lemon juice and
season with salt and pepper. Cook under a
moderately hot grill for about 5 minutes.
Turn the kebabs over, sprinkle with lemon
juice, salt, pepper and paprika pepper and
continue cooking until tender, about 3–5 minutes.
Make the tartare sauce by mixing all the
ingredients together.
Arrange the kebabs on a heated serving dish,
sprinkle with chopped parsley.
Serve the green salad and tartare sauce separately.

CURRIED COD   Dinner

Serves One

black pepper
2 teaspoons lemon juice
½ *pint chicken stock made with chicken stock cube and*
    water
8 oz. skinned cod fillet
1 tablespoon dried onion flakes
water
4 fl. oz. tomato juice
1 teaspoon curry powder
½ *teaspoon salt*
dash of Worcestershire sauce
peas or green salad for serving

Add pepper and lemon juice to the stock.
Place the prepared fish in an ovenproof dish.
Pour the seasoned stock over the fish and bake
in a moderately slow oven (325°F. Mark 3)
for about 10 minutes. Drain off the cooking
liquid. Soak the onion flakes until soft. Mix
together the tomato juice, onion flakes, curry
powder, salt, pepper and Worcestershire sauce
in a saucepan. Bring to the boil and pour over
the fish.
Serve with peas or a green salad.

COD STEAK TOLEDO   Dinner

Serves One

2 oz. skinned tomato
2 oz. button mushrooms
2 oz. onion
¼ *teaspoon salt*
freshly ground black pepper
8 oz. cod steak
chopped parsley for garnish

Chop the tomato and onion. Wash the
mushrooms and mix them with the tomato and
onion in a small bowl. Season.
Place the cod steak on a large square of foil in an
ovenproof dish. Pile the tomato mixture on top
and fold the foil over the top to make a parcel.
Bake in a hot oven (400°F. Mark 6) for about
30 minutes.
Just before serving, open the foil and sprinkle
the fish with chopped parsley.

COD KEBABS   Dinner

Serves Two

1 lb. cod steak
1 small green pepper
4 oz. button onions
4 oz. tomatoes
4 button mushrooms
4 small bay leaves
lemon juice
salt and freshly ground black pepper

NORWEGIAN FISH SALAD — Dinner

Serves Four

1½ lb. cooked white fish
2 sticks celery
1 canned red pepper
1 box of mustard and cress
4 tablespoons chicken stock made with chicken stock
    cube and water
1 tablespoon prepared mustard
1 tablespoon freshly grated horse-radish
4 tablespoons finely chopped watercress
4 tablespoons mayonnaise (optional)
4 large spinach leaves

Flake the fish and place in a bowl. Chop the celery and red pepper, wash the mustard and cress and cut off half the stems. Add the celery, pepper and mustard and cress to the fish with the stock, mustard, horse-radish, watercress and mayonnaise. Toss lightly.
Arrange the spinach leaves on a serving plate and pile the fish mixture on top. Chill before serving.

DUTCH LEMON COD — Dinner

Serves One

6–8 fl. oz. water
strips of rind of ¼ lemon
½ teaspoon salt
black pepper
1 × 8 oz. cod cutlet
lemon wedges and watercress for garnish

Place the water in a saucepan with the lemon rind, salt and black pepper. Bring to the boil, remove from the heat. Place fish in the saucepan, bring to the boil again and simmer gently until cooked, about 8–10 minutes.
Arrange the fish on a hot serving plate and garnish with lemon wedges and watercress.

WHITE FISH IN PIQUANT SAUCE — Lunch

Serves One

¼ teaspoon curry powder
salt and black pepper
1 tablespoon lemon juice
6 oz. white fish
1 medium-sized cooking apple
4 tablespoons cold water
⅓ chicken stock cube
3 drops artificial liquid sweetener
1 tablespoon lemon juice
1 tablespoon skimmed milk powder
cucumber slices for garnish
celery and cauliflower for serving

Sprinkle the curry powder, salt, pepper and lemon juice over the fish. Place on a piece of foil on a baking tray, cover and bake in the centre of a moderately slow oven (325°F, Mark 3) for about 20 minutes. Meanwhile peel, core and slice the apple and place in a saucepan with water and chicken stock cube and cook until reduced to a pulp.
Add the other ingredients and mix well together. Place the cooked fish on a serving dish and pour over the sauce. Garnish with slices of cucumber and serve with celery and cauliflower.

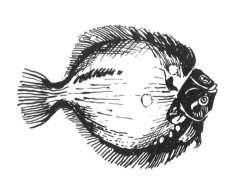

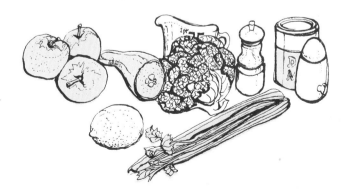

Norwegian Fish Salad (above)

Cod Kebabs (opposite top right)
Cod Steak Toledo (opposite bottom right)

ICELANDIC FISH
Lunch

Serves Two

12 oz. skinned cod
4 tablespoons skimmed milk
4 tablespoons tomato juice
salt and black pepper
2 slices bread, crumbed and toasted
2 inches cucumber
watercress for garnish

Cut the fish into small pieces and put it in layers
in a casserole. Cover with the milk and tomato
juice. Sprinkle with the seasonings and lightly
browned breadcrumbs. Cut the cucumber into
fairly thick slices and arrange in a single layer.
Cover and bake in the centre of a moderately
slow oven (325°F. Mark 3) for about 30
minutes. Drain off liquid.
Serve garnished with watercress.

BAKED HADDOCK
Dinner

Serves Two

1 lb. haddock
4 tablespoons wine vinegar
$\frac{1}{4}$ pint tomato juice
1 clove garlic, crushed
salt and black pepper
1 tablespoon chopped parsley
8 oz. cooked peas

Skin the haddock, cut it into two pieces and
place it in an ovenproof dish. Pour the wine
vinegar over the fish and cover with tomato
juice and garlic. Season well with salt, pepper
and parsley. Cover with foil and place in the
centre of a moderate oven (350°F. Mark 4)
for 20–25 minutes. Drain off the liquid. Serve
with cooked peas.

LEMON FISH SALAD

Lunch

Serves One

1 × 6 oz. cod or halibut steak
2 tablespoons lemon juice
2 tablespoons wine vinegar
1 head chicory
2 courgettes
½ red pepper
½ green pepper

Mayonnaise:
1 teaspoon dry mustard
2 tablespoons wine vinegar
½ oz. skimmed milk powder
little water
salt and black pepper
lettuce for serving

Place the fish in a saucepan with water to cover. Bring to the boil and simmer for about 10 minutes. Drain the fish and place in a shallow dish. Marinate the cooked fish overnight in the lemon juice and wine vinegar.
Slice the chicory and courgettes into ½ inch slices. Remove the seeds and membranes from the peppers and slice thinly. Place the mayonnaise ingredients in a screw-top jar and shake together until blended. Toss the chicory, courgettes and peppers in the mayonnaise.
Serve the fish on a bed of lettuce accompanied by the salad.

PORTUGUESE FISH

Lunch

Serves Two

1 × 6 oz. skinned haddock fillet
salt and black pepper
2 oz. finely grated Cheddar cheese
4 tablespoons skimmed milk
1 oz. fresh white breadcrumbs
2 teaspoons lemon juice
2 oz. button mushrooms
1 oz. breadcrumbs, toasted
lemon twists and parsley for garnish

Cut the fillet in half crosswise and place one piece in an ovenproof dish. Season well. Heat the cheese in half the milk, gently, remove from the heat and stir in the breadcrumbs and seasoning. Place the mixture on the fillet and cover with the remaining fish. Season again, sprinkle lemon juice over the fish and surround it with the washed mushrooms. Add the remaining milk and sprinkle the fish with toasted breadcrumbs. Cover with foil and bake in the centre of a moderately slow oven (325°F. Mark 3) for about 25 minutes. Drain off liquid.
Place on a hot serving plate and serve garnished with lemon twists and parsley.

POACHED HADDOCK WITH SALMON
Dinner

Serves Two

12 oz. fresh haddock
salt
4 oz. canned salmon
2 tablespoons mayonnaise

Court Bouillon:
1 bay leaf
3 teaspoons salt
3 peppercorns
1 tablespoon vinegar
1 pint water

Sprinkle the haddock with salt, leave for 15 minutes then rinse well. Place the fish in a piece of muslin.
Mix all the ingredients for the court bouillon in a saucepan, bring to the boil. Lower the haddock into the liquid, cover, bring back to the boil. Remove the pan from the heat and leave for about 15 minutes. Drain haddock very thoroughly on absorbent kitchen paper. Place on a heated serving dish.
Flake the salmon, place in a small non-stick saucepan and heat gently. Mix with the mayonnaise. Pile the salmon on top of the haddock and serve.

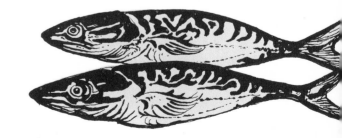

HALIBUT SPECIAL — Dinner

Serves Two

2 × 8 oz. halibut steaks
¼ teaspoon ground mace
½ teaspoon mixed dried sweet herbs
¼ pint skimmed milk

Place the halibut in a shallow ovenproof dish.
Mix the mace, herbs and skimmed milk
together and pour over the fish. Bake in a hot
oven (400°F. Mark 6) for about 15 minutes or
until the fish flakes easily with a fork.

HALIBUT WITH EGG AND LEMON SAUCE — Lunch

Serves Two

6 oz. skinned halibut
few strips of thinly peeled lemon rind
¼ pint skimmed milk
2 eggs
salt and black pepper
1 teaspoon lemon juice
1½ tablespoons chopped parsley
tomato wedges for garnish

Cook the prepared fish in a saucepan with
lightly salted water to cover for about 15
minutes. Place the lemon rind and skimmed milk
in a saucepan. Bring to the boil then remove
from the heat and leave for 10 minutes.
Whisk the eggs add the seasonings and lemon
juice and stir in the strained milk. Pour into the
top of a double saucepan (or bowl over a pan
of hot water) and heat gently, stirring
occasionally, until the sauce thickens. Stir in the
parsley.
Serve the fish on a hot plate and pour over the
lemon sauce. Garnish with tomato wedges.

GRILLED MACKEREL WITH GOOSEBERRY SAUCE — Dinner

Serves Two

2 × 10 oz. mackerel
salt and black pepper
2 teaspoons lemon juice
6 oz. green gooseberries
¼ pint water
artificial sweetener to taste
pinch of grated nutmeg
lemon wedges for garnish

Wash and clean the mackerel thoroughly.
Make 4 diagonal cuts across the sides. Season
both sides of the fish with salt, black pepper and
lemon juice. Place under a moderate grill and
cook for about 8–10 minutes turning once.
Meanwhile, make the gooseberry sauce by
stewing the prepared fruit in a saucepan with
the water until tender. Drain, then sieve or
blend to a purée. Add artificial sweetener and
grated nutmeg to taste.
Arrange the mackerel on a serving dish and
garnish with lemon wedges. Serve sauce
separately in a sauce boat.

QUICKIE FISH CAKES — Dinner

Serves One

1 teaspoon dried onion flakes
¼ teaspoon Tabasco sauce
½ teaspoon Worcestershire sauce
½ teaspoon soy sauce
6 oz. cooked hake
3 teaspoons prepared mustard
1 teaspoon finely chopped parsley
salt to taste

Tartare Sauce:
1 tablespoon mayonnaise
½ teaspoon chopped capers
½ teaspoon chopped gherkin
½ teaspoon finely chopped parsley

Mix the onion flakes with the three sauces and
leave for 15 minutes or until the onion is
softened. Flake the hake and mix with the
onion and sauces, mustard, parsley and salt.
Beat well and shape into two flat cakes. Heat a
non-stick frying pan and cook the fish cakes
until golden, turning once.
Mix all the ingredients for the tartare sauce
together thoroughly.
Serve the fish cakes on a heated serving plate
with the tartare sauce.

MACKEREL MOUSSE Lunch

Serves Two

8 oz. canned mackerel fillets
8 fl. oz. tomato juice
¼ teaspoon wine vinegar
pinch of salt and black pepper
dash of Tabasco sauce
dash of Worcestershire sauce
½ oz. gelatine
2 tablespoons water
3–4 small gherkins
lemon slices and parsley for garnish

Drain the mackerel fillets and remove the skin
and any bones. Place in an electric blender with
the tomato juice, vinegar, salt, black pepper,
Tabasco sauce and Worcestershire sauce. Blend
at high speed for 30 seconds.
Dissolve the gelatine in water over a pan of hot
water and stir into the puréed fish mixture.
Pour into a ½ pint soufflé dish and leave in a
cool place to set.
Serve garnished with lemon slices and parsley
sprigs.

PICKLED MACKEREL Dinner

Serves Six

6 × 10 oz. mackerel
salt and pepper
1 tablespoon dried onion flakes
8 fl. oz. white wine vinegar
2 tablespoons water
1 clove garlic (optional)
1 blade mace
green salad for serving

Clean and bone the mackerel, cut off the heads
and tails. Season well with salt and pepper and
roll the fish up, secure with a wooden cocktail
stick. Arrange the rolled mackerel in a shallow
ovenproof dish, sprinkle with the onion flakes
and add the vinegar, water, garlic and mace.
Cover the dish with foil and cook in a slow
oven (300°F. Mark 2) for 1½ hours.
Cool before eating. This dish improves with
keeping, place the fish in a lidded jar, pour over
the cooled cooking liquid and keep for up to
2 weeks.
Arrange a salad on a serving plate and place
the fish on top.

MACKEREL IN FOIL Dinner

Serves Two

2 × 10 oz. mackerel
½ teaspoon salt
freshly ground black pepper
4 oz. tomato
½ lemon
parsley for garnish

Cut and clean the fish, leave on the tail. Season
well with salt and black pepper. Place each fish
on a piece of foil in an ovenproof dish.
Skin the tomato and slice. Slice the lemon
thinly. Arrange alternate slices of tomato and
lemon on the fish. Fold the foil over the top and
seal to make a neat parcel. Bake in a moderate
oven (350°F. Mark 4) for 25–30 minutes.
Open the foil before serving and garnish each
fish with a sprig of parsley.

HOT SPICY MACKEREL Dinner

Serves One

1 × 10 oz. mackerel
2 teaspoons lemon juice
½ teaspoon ground turmeric
¼ teaspoon chilli powder
½ teaspoon black pepper
salt
¼ teaspoon garlic salt (optional)

Wash and clean the mackerel. Cut across the
sides of the fish 4 times with a sharp knife on
both sides. Mix the lemon juice with the rest of
the ingredients in a bowl to make a paste.
Brush the fish with the paste inside and out,
brushing well inside the slits. Place the fish on a
piece of foil and leave to marinate for 15
minutes. Bake in a moderate oven (350°F.
Mark 4) for about 15 minutes.
Drain off liquid, place fish on a serving plate and
garnish with lemon twists.

Mackerel in Foil (opposite top)

Pickled Mackerel (opposite bottom)

CUCUMBER PLAICE   Dinner

Serves One

1 × 10 oz. skinned plaice
2 teaspoons finely chopped parsley
¼ cucumber
juice of ½ lemon
¼ teaspoon salt
black pepper
chopped parsley for garnish

Wipe the fish and place it in a casserole, sprinkle
with chopped parsley and arrange thin slices of
cucumber on top. Sprinkle with lemon juice,
salt and black pepper. Place in a moderately slow
oven (325°F. Mark 3) for about 30–40 minutes.
Drain off the liquid.
Serve garnished with chopped parsley.

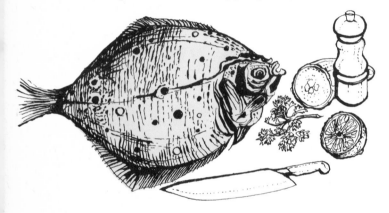

TARAMASALATA   Lunch

Serves Two

8 oz. canned mackerel fillets
1 tablespoon water
2 tablespoons lemon juice
2 gherkins
1 inch cucumber
dash of Worcestershire sauce
salt and black pepper
lemon twists and parsley for garnish

Drain the fish and break it into rough flakes.
Put it in a blender with the water and lemon
juice. Blend at high speed until smooth. Pour the
mixture into a bowl and stir in the chopped
gherkins and cucumber. Add a dash of
Worcestershire sauce. Taste and adjust the
seasoning.
Pour into a serving dish and chill in the
refrigerator for a few hours. Serve garnished
with lemon twists and parsley.

GRILLED SALMON   Dinner

Serves Four

4 × 8 oz. fresh salmon steaks
2 tablespoons chicken stock made with chicken stock
  cube and water
paprika pepper
2 tablespoons cider vinegar
4 lemon wedges
watercress for garnish
4 tablespoons mayonnaise

Place the salmon steaks in a grill pan and pour
over 1 tablespoon stock, and 1 tablespoon cider
vinegar. Sprinkle with a little paprika pepper.
Cook under a hot grill, about 3 inches away, for
5 minutes. Turn the salmon over, pour over the
remaining 1 tablespoon each stock and cider
vinegar and sprinkle with paprika pepper.
Grill for a further 5 minutes or until the fish
flakes easily with a fork.
Arrange the salmon steaks on a serving dish.
Garnish each one with a lemon wedge and a
sprig of parsley. Serve the mayonnaise separately,
or place a tablespoon of mayonnaise on top of
each steak.

SALMON IN PAPER   Lunch

Serves Two

2 × 6 oz. salmon steaks
2 teaspoons chopped parsley
2 oz. breadcrumbs
2 tablespoons skimmed milk
salt and black pepper
lemon wedges for garnish
green salad for serving

Trim and wipe the salmon steaks. Mix the
parsley and breadcrumbs with milk in a bowl,
season with salt and black pepper. Divide this
mixture into 4, place half of this mixture on two
pieces of foil on a baking sheet and spread out.
Place the salmon steaks on top of the stuffing
mixture, and spread the rest of the stuffing over
the top of the steaks. Fold the foil over and bake
in the centre of a moderately slow oven
(325°F. Mark 3) for about 20–30 minutes.
Arrange the salmon on a serving dish and
garnish with lemon wedges.
Serve a green salad separately.

SALMON SAVOURIES   Lunch

Serves Two

8 oz. canned salmon
2 oz. wholemeal breadcrumbs
2 teaspoons finely chopped parsley
grated rind of ½ lemon
1 tablespoon lemon juice
1 tablespoon tomato juice
dash of Worcestershire sauce
salt and black pepper
green salad for serving

Drain the salmon, place in a bowl and flake.
Mix with the breadcrumbs, parsley and lemon
rind. Moisten with lemon juice and tomato
juice. Season with Worcestershire sauce, salt,
and pepper. Shape into patties and cook gently
in a non-stick frying pan until brown on the top,
bottom and sides, about 20 minutes. Serve with
a green salad.

BAKED LEMON SOLE   Dinner

Serves Four

2 lb. fresh lemon sole fillets
2 tablespoons lemon juice
2 tablespoons salt
¼ teaspoon white pepper
1 tablespoon grated orange rind
2 teaspoons grated lemon rind

Tartare Sauce:
4 tablespoons mayonnaise
2 teaspoons chopped capers
2 teaspoons chopped gherkins
1 teaspoon finely chopped parsley

Brush the sole fillets all over with lemon juice
and season on both sides with salt and pepper.
Place the fillets in an ovenproof dish and sprinkle
with the grated orange rind and lemon rind.
Cook in a hot oven (400°F. Mark 6) for
10 minutes or until the fish flakes easily with a
fork.

SKATE WITH ORANGE   Dinner

Serves Two

1 tablespoon salt
1 quart water
3 tablespoons vinegar
bouquet garni
6 peppercorns
1¼ lb. skate
4 oz. onion, sliced
1 orange
3 tablespoons low calorie orange squash
1 teaspoon wine vinegar
salt and black pepper
1 teaspoon chopped parsley
1 teaspoon dried thyme
watercress for garnish

Prepare a court bouillon by dissolving the salt
in the water in a large saucepan. Add the
vinegar, bouquet garni and peppercorns.
Bring to the boil and boil for 5 minutes.
Leave to cool. Cut the skate into 4 portions and
place it in a large saucepan. Strain the court
bouillon and pour it on to the fish. Bring
slowly to boiling point, cover the pan and
simmer for about 20 minutes. Meanwhile,
prepare a sauce by frying the sliced onion
gently in a non-stick frying pan until soft.
Peel the orange and cut into ¼ inch slices.
Add the orange squash, vinegar, seasoning and
herbs to the cooked onion. Bring to the boil,
add the orange slices and simmer gently.
Arrange the cooked skate in a serving dish.
Pour the prepared sauce over the fish and
garnish with sprigs of watercress.

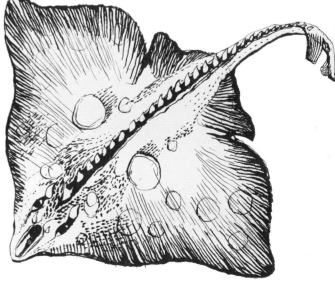

CRISPY SOLE

Lunch

Serves Two

12 oz. Dover sole fillets
pinch of salt
black pepper
⅓ pint skimmed milk
2 oz. breadcrumbs
lemon wedges and tomato slices for garnish

Tartare Sauce:
2 tablespoons mayonnaise
1 teaspoon finely chopped peppers
1 teaspoon finely chopped gherkins
1 teaspoon chopped parsley

Skin and wipe the sole fillets. Season well.
Cut each fillet into ½ inch strips diagonally.
Dip each piece of fish into the milk and roll
in breadcrumbs, patting the coating on firmly.
Grill for 5–7 minutes, turning once. Transfer to a
serving dish and keep warm.
To make the sauce, mix all the ingredients
together in a bowl. Serve the fish with tartare
sauce, garnished with lemon wedges and tomato
slices.

SOLE CECILIA

Lunch

Serves Two

6 oz. sole fillets
8 asparagus tips
4 thin lemon slices
salt and black pepper
2 oz. grated cheese
tomato slices, watercress, lemon wedges for garnish

Skin and wipe the sole fillets. Place them on a
piece of foil. Divide asparagus tips equally
between fillets and place the tips on top of the
fish. Cut the lemon slices in half and place them
across the length of the fish. Season with salt
and black pepper. Fold up the foil to make a
parcel and bake in the centre of a moderate
oven (350°F. Mark 4) for about 20–25 minutes.
Drain off the cooking liquid, remove the lemon
slices and sprinkle with grated cheese. Place
under the grill to brown. Transfer to a serving
plate and serve garnished with tomato slices,
watercress and lemon wedges.

STUFFED RAINBOW TROUT

Lunch

Serves Four

4 × 8 oz. trout
1 small green pepper
1 small red pepper
4 oz. mushrooms
2 teaspoons dried onion flakes
pinch of mixed dried herbs
pinch of dry mustard
salt and pepper
lettuce and cress for serving
lemon for garnish

Clean the trout, remove the seeds and
membranes from the peppers and chop. Wash
and chop the mushrooms. Place the peppers
and mushrooms in a bowl, add the onion flakes,
herbs, mustard, salt and pepper. Mix well.
Stuff the trout with the pepper mixture. Place
on a piece of foil in an ovenproof dish and
put any extra stuffing around the fish.
Fold the foil over the trout and seal. Bake in a
moderate oven (350°F. Mark 4) for about
30 minutes.
Arrange a bed of lettuce on a serving plate, put
the trout on top and place a little cress at each
end.
Serve garnished with lemon slices.

TUNA FISH SALAD

Lunch

Serves Two

4 oz. canned tuna
2 hard-boiled eggs
1 tablespoon dried onion flakes
2 tablespoons mayonnaise
salt and black pepper
2 teaspoons lemon juice
lettuce leaves for serving
tomato, toast and celery for garnishing

Drain the tuna well and place it in a bowl.
Chop the eggs, soak the onion until softened.
Mix the eggs and onion flakes with the tuna,
mayonnaise and season well. Sprinkle with
lemon juice.
Arrange the lettuce on a serving platter.
Garnish with tomato slices, toast triangles and
celery curls.

Stuffed Rainbow Trout (opposite top)

Tuna Salad in Orange Cups (opposite bottom)

TUNA SALAD IN ORANGE CUPS Lunch

Serves Two

2 large oranges
8 oz. drained canned tuna
2 sticks celery
2 tablespoons chopped cucumber
1 tablespoon chopped canned red pepper
½ tablespoon Worcestershire sauce
1 tablespoon tomato juice
2 tablespoons mayonnaise (optional)
salt and freshly ground black pepper
parsley for garnish

Cut the tops off the oranges about one third of
the way down from the top. Scallop the edge if
desired. Carefully scoop out the flesh, without
damaging the orange skin, and cut up. Flake the
tuna, slice the celery thinly and combine in a
bowl with the chopped orange, cucumber, red
pepper, Worcestershire sauce, tomato juice,
mayonnaise. Season to taste.
Spoon the tuna mixture into the orange skins,
place the 'lid' on top and garnish with a sprig
of parsley.

SOLE IN WINE SAUCE Lunch

Serves Two

2 × 6 oz. fillets of Dover sole
4 oz. button mushrooms
2 tablespoons cooked cauliflower
1 teaspoon dried onion flakes
1 teaspoon chopped parsley
salt and black pepper
½ oz. skimmed milk powder
1 tablespoon water
2 tablespoons white wine vinegar
1 × 12 oz. packet frozen spinach

Wipe the fillets and skin. Chop the mushrooms
finely. Place half the mushrooms in a bowl with
the cauliflower, onion flakes, parsley and
seasoning, mix well. Spread the stuffing on the
fillets and roll them up. Place on a piece of foil
on a baking sheet and cover with more foil.
Bake in the centre of a moderate oven (350°F.
Mark 4) for about 25 minutes.
For the wine sauce, blend the milk powder with
the water and wine vinegar in a bowl. Add the
remaining mushrooms, salt and pepper. Stand
the bowl in a pan of hot water and cook,
stirring occasionally, until sauce thickens.
Put in an electric blender at high speed for
30 seconds. Pour into a sauce boat. Cook the
spinach as directed on the packet.

Drain and arrange on a serving dish. Arrange the
stuffed fish on the bed of spinach and serve with
the wine sauce.

TUNA SURPRISE Lunch

Serves One

4 oz. canned tuna
2 oz. pimento
2 oz. frozen runner beans
pinch of curry powder
½ teaspoon salt
black pepper
1 slice of toast, cut into triangles for serving

Put tuna fish, chopped pimento, thawed runner
beans, curry powder, salt and pepper into a
non-stick saucepan. Cover the pan and cook
gently for 10 minutes.
Serve with the triangles of toast arranged
around the dish.

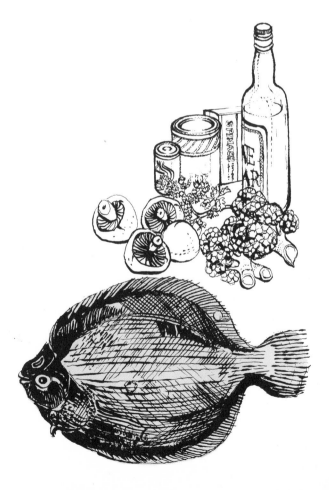

PRAWNS WITH CHEESE   Lunch

Serves One

1 oz. grated Cheddar cheese
2 teaspoons skimmed milk
2 oz. prawns
1 slice bread
chopped parsley for garnish

Melt the cheese in the milk in a small saucepan over a low heat. Stir in the prawns and heat through slowly for about 10 minutes. Toast the slice of bread and pile the prawn mixture on the toast. Sprinkle with chopped parsley. Serve immediately.

PRAWN ITALIENNE   Lunch

Serves Two

5 fl. oz. tomato juice
8 oz. prawns
2 teaspoons lemon juice
dash of Worcestershire sauce
salt and black pepper
green salad for serving

Pour the tomato juice over the prawns in a shallow dish. Stir in the lemon juice, Worcestershire sauce and seasonings. Marinate for two hours and serve with a green salad.

SHRIMP CHOW MEIN   Dinner

Serves Two

1 green pepper
3 oz. button mushrooms
2 sticks celery
2 teaspoons dried onion flakes
12 fl. oz. tomato juice
salt and pepper
1 tablespoon soy sauce
1 teaspoon lemon juice
$\frac{1}{2} \times 16$ oz. can bean sprouts
12 oz. canned or frozen shrimps

Remove the seeds and membranes from the pepper and slice finely. Finely slice the mushrooms and celery. Place the prepared vegetables in a saucepan with the onion flakes, tomato juice, salt and pepper, soy sauce and lemon juice. Bring to the boil, stirring, cover and simmer for 10 minutes.
Stir in the bean sprouts and shrimps and reheat, stirring, for about 3 minutes. Adjust seasoning and serve.

KING-CRAB SPECIAL   Dinner

Serves Two

2 sticks celery
$\frac{1}{4}$ pint plus 4 tablespoons chicken stock made with stock cube and water
2 tablespoons lemon juice
about 1 teaspoon almond essence
12 oz. king-crab
green salad for serving

Slice celery into $\frac{1}{4}$ inch pieces, place in a bowl and add the stock, lemon juice and almond essence. Mix together then leave for 1 hour. Place the celery mixture in a saucepan, add the crab and cook gently, stirring, until hot. Serve a green salad separately.

COQUILLES ST. JACQUES   Lunch

Serves Two

4 oz. cooked scallops or shrimps
2 oz. mushrooms
$\frac{1}{4}$ pint plus 1 tablespoon skimmed milk
2 teaspoons dried onion flakes
pinch of garlic powder
salt and pepper
6 oz. cooked potato
2 oz. finely grated cheese
2 oz. breadcrumbs

Chop the scallops. Wash and chop the mushrooms, cook in a saucepan of boiling water for 2 minutes, drain well. Place the scallops, mushrooms, $\frac{1}{4}$ pint skimmed milk, onion flakes, garlic powder, salt and pepper in a saucepan. Reheat.
Mash the potato with the remaining 1 tablespoon skimmed milk and arrange it as a border around deep scallop shells or small serving dishes. Mix the cheese with the breadcrumbs. Sprinkle half of the breadcrumb mixture on the base of the shells, spoon the scallop mixture on top. Sprinkle the remaining breadcrumb mixture on the top. Cook in a moderate oven (350°F. Mark 4) for 15–20 minutes or until the tops are beginning to brown.
Note: Cook the scallops by poaching them gently in skimmed milk for 5 minutes.

Coquilles St. Jacques (top p. 58)

Shrimp Chow Mein (bottom p. 58)

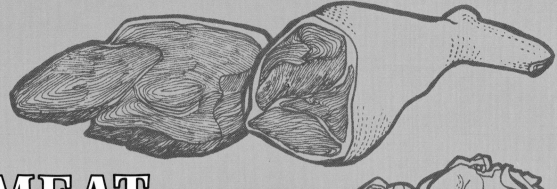

MEAT

The Weight Watchers Programme of Eating does not allow you to cook *anything*, and that includes meat, with fat or oil. So you will find a non-stick pan useful for dry frying. Before cooking, remove all visible fat. As for the juices which seep from the meat during cooking, these must always be drained before the meat is served. Then you simply add a Weight Watchers gravy or sauce. Because the Programme is a normal way of eating it fits easily into normal life and the everyday commitments of a housewife feeding her family. For example, if your family are having a fattening sauce, you remove your meat from the casserole before adding the thickening. There is no need at all to make a separate meal.

Spice up the Sunday joint:

BEEF, sprinkle with salt and freshly ground black pepper and soy sauce or Worcestershire sauce before rack roasting.

LAMB, before roasting insert four slivers of garlic into the skin of the joint and rub 1 teaspoon dry mustard into the skin.

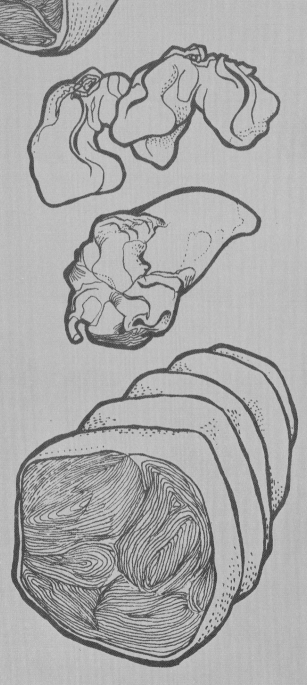

59

BEEFBURGER SAUSAGES　　　Dinner

Serves Four

2 lbs. minced beef
4 oz. grated onion
4 oz. grated carrot
1 clove garlic, crushed
1 chicken stock cube
1 teaspoon salt
pinch of pepper
4 oz. fresh white breadcrumbs
$\frac{1}{4}$ teaspoon paprika pepper
parsley for garnish

Place the minced beef in a bowl with the onion, carrot, garlic, stock cube, salt and pepper.
Mix very thoroughly. Form into small sausages about $\frac{3}{4}$ inch diameter and 2–3 inches long.
Mix the breadcrumbs with the paprika pepper. Roll each sausage in breadcrumbs until well coated.
Place the sausages on a rack in a grill pan and cook under a hot grill, turning frequently until browned all over and cooked.
Serve piled on to a hot plate, garnished with a sprig of parsley.

BEEF CASSEROLE　　　Dinner

Serves Two

1 lb. lean stewing steak
$\frac{1}{2}$ pint tomato juice
2 teaspoons dried onion flakes
$\frac{1}{4}$ teaspoon mixed dried herbs
salt and black pepper
2 beef stock cubes
chopped parsley for garnish

Trim off any fat from the meat and cut into 1 inch cubes. Place the meat in a casserole, combine the tomato juice with the onion flakes, herbs, seasoning and beef stock cubes and pour over the meat in the casserole. Cover and cook in the centre of a moderately slow oven (325°F. Mark 3) for about 2 hours. Drain off the liquid and serve garnished with chopped parsley.

BEEFSTEAK IN MUSHROOM SAUCE
　　　　　　　　　　　　　　Dinner

Serves One

1×8 oz. Porterhouse steak
salt and black pepper
1 clove garlic, crushed
2 oz. button mushrooms
$\frac{1}{4}$ pint tomato juice
$\frac{1}{2}$ teaspoon dried oregano
chopped parsley
cauliflower or celery for serving

Wipe the steak, season and place it under a hot grill until cooked, turning once. Remove from the grill and keep warm on a serving plate. Place the garlic, chopped mushrooms and tomato juice in a small saucepan and cook for about 3 minutes. Add the oregano and cook for a further few minutes.
Pour the sauce over cooked steak. Serve garnished with chopped parsley accompanied by freshly cooked cauliflower or celery.

GOULASH　　　Dinner

Serves Two

12 oz. cooked chuck steak
salt and black pepper
$1\frac{1}{2}$ pints beef stock made with beef stock cube and water
8 oz. onions, sliced
$\frac{1}{2}$ pint tomato juice
1 tablespoon lemon juice
$1\frac{1}{2}$ teaspoons paprika pepper
$\frac{1}{2}$ medium-sized fresh pineapple, chopped
chopped parsley for garnish

Cut the steak into 1 inch cubes, season well with salt and black pepper. Combine the rest of the ingredients in a saucepan and simmer for about 40 minutes. Add the meat to the saucepan and simmer until meat is heated thoroughly.
Pour into a serving dish and garnish with chopped parsley.

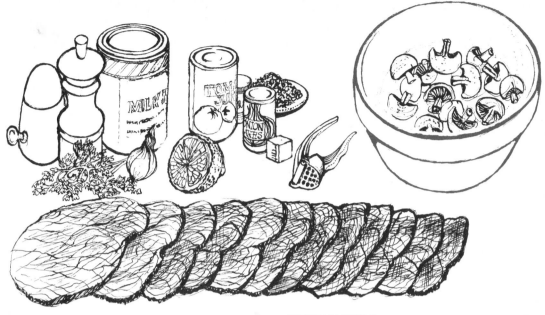

BEEF STROGANOFF   Lunch

Serves Two

12 oz. topside or rump steak
salt and black pepper
2 tablespoons dried onion flakes
3 oz. button mushrooms
2 teaspoons tomato juice
$\frac{1}{3}$ pint beef stock made with beef stock cube and water
pinch of grated nutmeg
$\frac{1}{2}$ teaspoon made mustard
2 oz. skimmed milk powder
water
1 teaspoon lemon juice
mustard and cress for garnish
green salad for serving

Trim off fat and cut the meat into $\frac{1}{4}$ inch strips.
Season it with salt and pepper. Line the grill pan
with foil and place the seasoned meat on the foil.
Grill the meat gently, turning frequently until
cooked. Soak the onions, slice the mushrooms
and fry gently in a non-stick saucepan for about
4 minutes. Add the tomato juice, stock, nutmeg
and mustard. Bring to the boil, cover and
simmer for about 10 minutes. Mix the milk
powder with enough water to make a cream
mixture with the lemon juice. Blend a little of
the stock into the soured cream. Pour back into
the stock and add the drained cooked meat.
Reheat for about 10 minutes, but do not boil.
Pour into a serving dish and garnish with cress.
Serve with a green salad.

BEEF ROLLS   Lunch

Serves Two

12 × 1 oz. slices of grilling steak
2 oz. button mushrooms
2 tablespoons dried onion flakes
2 tablespoons skimmed milk powder
1 teaspoon grated lemon rind
juice of $\frac{1}{2}$ lemon
2 oz. breadcrumbs
2 teaspoons parsley
2 tablespoons water
salt and black pepper
watercress for garnish

Sauce:
8 fl. oz. tomato juice
1 beef stock cube
1 clove garlic, crushed
1$\frac{1}{2}$ teaspoons French mustard

Trim fat off the steak slices. Wash and chop the
mushrooms. Soak the onion flakes until
softened. Mix together the mushrooms with the
onion in a bowl, add the milk powder, lemon
peel and juice, breadcrumbs, parsley and water
and mix. Season well. Divide the stuffing
equally between the beef slices, roll up and
secure with wooden cocktail sticks. Grill
slowly, turning frequently for about 20 minutes,
until cooked.
Make the sauce by combining the tomato juice
with the beef stock cube in a saucepan, then add
the crushed garlic and mustard. Season and
simmer for 15 minutes.
Arrange the rolls on a serving plate and pour
over the sauce. Garnish with watercress.

61

Beefburger Sausages (above)

Steak Roll (opposite top right)

Stuffed Cabbage Rolls (opposite bottom right)

MARINATED BEEF   Dinner

Serves Four

2 lb. beef rump or sirloin tip
8 fl. oz. vinegar
8 fl. oz. water
4 oz. onion
1 lemon
5 cloves
2 bay leaves
3 black peppercorns
1 tablespoon salt
artificial sweetener to equal 1 tablespoon sugar

Place the meat in a deep bowl. Pour the
vinegar and water over the meat. Add the other
ingredients and cover. Turn the meat two or
three times and leave overnight in the
refrigerator.
Drain the meat and place it on a rack in a
roasting pan. Add ½ pint of the marinade to the
roasting pan. Cook the meat in a moderate
oven (350°F. Mark 4) for about 45 minutes.
Baste the meat with the marinade; turn
occasionally during cooking.

SPRING THYME MINCE   Dinner

Serves One

8 oz. lean minced beef
½ teaspoon dried thyme
2 teaspoons dried onion flakes
1 teaspoon lemon juice
2 teaspoons curry powder
about ½ pint tomato juice
4 oz. cooked spaghetti

Heat a heavy-based non-stick saucepan, add the
minced beef and cook over a gentle heat,
stirring constantly, until the meat is browned.
Pour off all liquid. Add the thyme, onion flakes,
lemon juice and curry powder and just cover
with tomato juice. Simmer for 20 minutes,
adding more tomato juice as necessary.
Arrange the hot, freshly-cooked spaghetti on a
serving plate and spoon the meat on top.
Note: This recipe can also be used for stuffing
marrow or green peppers.

STEAK ROLL   Dinner

Serves Two

1 lb. braising steak in one flat piece
2 tablespoons dried onion flakes
4 oz. mushrooms
1 tomato
1 clove garlic, crushed
1 tablespoon beef stock made with beef stock cube
    and water
made mustard
freshly ground black pepper
salt
$\frac{1}{4}$ teaspoon mixed dried herbs

Place the beef between two sheets of polythene
and beat well with a rolling pin or meat mallet
until about $\frac{1}{4}$ inch thick.
Soak the onion flakes until softened. Wash and
chop the mushrooms. Plunge the tomato into a
saucepan of boiling water for 1 minute, rinse in
cold water, skin and chop. Mix all the prepared
vegetables together in a bowl with the garlic and
beef stock.
Spread the steak thinly with made mustard then
season well with freshly ground black pepper
and salt. Sprinkle with the herbs. Cover the
steak with the vegetable mixture. Roll up the
steak like a Swiss roll and secure with skewers.
Wrap the roll in foil, place it on a baking tray
and bake in a moderately hot oven (375°F.
Mark 5) for $1\frac{1}{4}$ hours. Remove the foil from the
top of the roll for the last 20 minutes to allow it
to brown. Drain off any liquid.
Serve cut into 1 inch slices.

VEAL IN FOIL   Dinner

Serves One

8 oz. slice of lean veal
4 tablespoons chopped mushrooms
2 tablespoons chopped parsley
2 tablespoons dried onion flakes
1 tablespoon chopped chives
salt and black pepper
mustard and cress for garnish

Trim the veal. Mix the rest of the ingredients
together in a bowl and spread half of this
mixture on a sheet of foil. Place the veal on top
and cover with the rest of the mixture. Fold over
the foil to make a parcel and cook in the centre
of a moderate oven (350°F. Mark 4) for about
1 hour. Drain off any liquid.
Arrange on a serving dish garnished with
mustard and cress.

SUMMER BEEF SALAD   Lunch

Serves Two

8 oz. cold roast beef
1 dessert apple
2 teaspoons lemon juice
1 stick celery
2 tablespoons button mushrooms
1 small clove garlic, crushed
2 teaspoons chopped parsley
salt and black pepper
1-2 tablespoons wine vinegar
tomato and watercress for garnish

Trim the fat off the meat and dice. Peel, core
and dice the apple and sprinkle with lemon
juice to prevent discoloration. Dice the celery,
chop the mushrooms and combine the diced
beef, apples, celery, mushrooms, garlic and
parsley in a bowl. Season with salt, pepper and
add the vinegar. Toss together. Arrange on a
serving plate garnished with tomato slices and
watercress.

VEAL AND EGG SALAD   Lunch

Serves One

$\frac{1}{2}$ pint chicken stock made with chicken stock cube
    and water
2 teaspoons gelatine
$\frac{1}{2}$ teaspoon mixed dried herbs
$\frac{1}{2}$ teaspoon lemon juice
few drops green food colouring
2 oz. cooked minced veal
salt and freshly ground black pepper
1 hard-boiled egg
watercress
chicory leaves and radishes for garnish

Heat the stock until almost boiling, add the
gelatine and stir until dissolved. Add the herbs,
lemon juice and green colouring.
Place the veal in a bowl, add the gelatine
mixture, salt and pepper and mix thoroughly.
Place one third of the veal mixture in a small
mould and put in a cool place until set. Place the
hard-boiled egg on top and cover with the
remaining veal. Put in a cool place until set.
Arrange a bed of watercress on a serving plate.
Unmould the veal, cut in half lengthwise and
place both halves on the watercress. Garnish
with chicory and radishes.

VIENNESE BEEFBURGERS   Dinner

Serves Two

16 oz. minced beef
1 teaspoon chopped parsley
$\frac{1}{4}$ teaspoon mixed dried herbs
$\frac{1}{2}$ teaspoon salt
black pepper
$\frac{1}{4}$ pint skimmed milk
4 oz. chopped onion
pinch of ground mace
salt and black pepper
4 oz. cooked peas and carrots for serving

Put the minced beef in a bowl, add the parsley and mixed herbs, season with salt and pepper, mix thoroughly together and shape into 4 flat cakes. Cook these under a moderately hot grill, turning once only, for 8–10 minutes.
To make the sauce, place the onion in the skimmed milk and simmer until tender, add the mace and seasonings and simmer for a further 5 minutes. Sieve or blend the onion sauce and serve with beefburgers.
Serve freshly cooked peas and carrots separately.

rolls in a shallow ovenproof dish, pour over the remaining stock and the tomato juice.
Cook in a hot oven (400°F. Mark 6) for 25–30 minutes.
Serve the rolls sprinkled with lemon juice.

STUFFED CABBAGE ROLLS   Dinner

Serves Four

8 large cabbage leaves
1$\frac{1}{2}$ lb. minced cooked beef
1 tablespoon dried onion flakes
2 teaspoons chopped parsley
2 teaspoons chopped chives
salt and pepper
$\frac{3}{4}$ pint chicken stock made with chicken stock cube
*   and water*
3 tablespoons tomato juice
juice of $\frac{1}{2}$ lemon

Cook the cabbage leaves in boiling salted water for 3–4 minutes. Drain and rinse in cold water.
Put the beef in a bowl with the onion flakes, parsley and chives, salt and pepper. Mix well, adding a little of the chicken stock to moisten the mixture slightly.
Divide the meat mixture into 8 portions and place one in the centre of each cabbage leaf. Fold the leaves to enclose the meat, folding in the sides to make neat parcels. Place the cabbage

STUFFED MARROW   Lunch

Serves Two

2 small marrows
salt
8 oz. cooked minced beef
2 oz. breadcrumbs
1 tablespoon dried onion flakes
dash of Worcestershire sauce
salt and black pepper
8 fl. oz. tomato juice
watercress for garnish

Cut the tops off the marrows to make lids. Scoop out the seeds. Sprinkle the marrows with salt and leave to stand for about 1 hour. Meanwhile, combine the minced beef, breadcrumbs, soaked onion flakes and seasonings together and bind with 8 fl. oz. of the tomato juice.
Drain the marrows well and dry on absorbent kitchen paper. Place the beef mixture down the centre of the marrows and place them in an ovenproof dish. Pour over the remaining tomato juice, replace the 'lids' and cover.
Bake in the centre of a moderate oven (350°F. Mark 4) for 1–1$\frac{1}{4}$ hours.
Serve hot, garnished with watercress.

Herb Baked Breast of Veal (opposite)　　　　　*Veal and Egg Salad (above)*

HERB BAKED BREAST OF VEAL

Dinner

Serves Four

1 × 2 lb. breast of veal
1 medium-sized cauliflower
1 can French green beans
1 can mushrooms
¼ pint chicken stock made from stock cube and water
1 tablespoon soy sauce
salt and black pepper
½ stick celery
4 tablespoons dried onion flakes
2 cloves garlic, crushed
⅛ teaspoon dried thyme
½ bay leaf, crushed
½ teaspoon chopped fresh parsley
½ teaspoon rosemary
¼ pint water

Ask your butcher to bone and trim the veal and make a pocket in the side. Cook the cauliflower in boiling salted water until tender. Drain and mash well. Drain the canned beans and mushrooms, put into a bowl with the cauliflower, stock, soy sauce, salt and pepper. Mix thoroughly then stuff the veal breast. Sew up the opening with fine string. Sprinkle the meat with salt and pepper and place on rack in roasting pan, boned side up. Chop the celery coarsely and sprinkle it over the veal with the onion flakes, garlic, thyme, bay leaf, parsley and rosemary. Roast in a moderate oven (350°F. Mark 4) for 15 minutes. Turn the veal over and cook for a further 45 minutes, basting frequently. Add the ¼ pint water to the pan, cover with foil and continue baking for 30 minutes. Remove the foil for the last 8 minutes. Place the meat on a serving plate. Remove the string.

67

VEAL LOUISA Dinner

Serves Four

2 lb. stewing veal
1 teaspoon paprika pepper
1 teaspoon salt
black pepper
2 teaspoons Worcestershire sauce
11 fl. oz. chicken stock made with water and chicken stock cube
1 clove garlic, crushed
2 oz. skimmed milk powder
water
1 teaspoon lemon juice
chopped parsley for garnish

Cut the meat into 1 inch cubes, toss in paprika, salt and pepper. Fry meat gently in a non-stick saucepan. When lightly browned, add the Worcestershire sauce, 6 fl. oz. stock and garlic. Bring to the boil, cover pan and simmer gently for about 1½ hours. Drain off the cooking liquid. Pour the remaining ¼ pint of chicken stock into a bowl. Put the milk powder into a bowl, add enough water to make a cream and then add the lemon juice. Stir the 'soured cream' into the stock. Pour into the saucepan and heat gently without boiling.
Place in a serving dish and serve garnished with chopped parsley.

VEAL PLATTER Dinner

Serves Two

1 lb. stewing veal
1 pint water
1 bay leaf
strips of lemon rind
salt and black pepper
¼ oz. gelatine
2 tablespoons water
¾ pint chicken stock made with chicken stock cube and water
2 tablespoons lemon juice
1 teaspoon paprika pepper
¼ teaspoon dried marjoram
1 chicken stock cube
sliced tomatoes and 8 oz. cooked peas for garnish
green salad for serving

Cut the veal into 1 inch cubes and place in a saucepan with the water, bay leaf, lemon rind, salt and black pepper. Bring to the boil and simmer for about 1½ hours or until tender. Drain off the cooking liquid, remove the bay leaf, lemon rind and chop the veal thoroughly. Dissolve the gelatine in water over a pan of hot water. When dissolved, stir into the stock and add the lemon juice, paprika, marjoram and the crumbled stock cube.
Arrange the well seasoned veal in a wetted 1½ pint ring mould; pour on the stock. Leave to set.
Unmould the veal on a serving dish. Garnish with sliced tomatoes and peas. Serve with a green salad.

VEAL MARENGO — Dinner

Serves Two

12 oz. cooked veal
½ pint chicken stock made with chicken stock cube
   and water
½ pint tomato juice
1 tablespoon dried onion flakes
salt and pepper
¼ teaspoon garlic powder
¼ teaspoon paprika pepper
4 oz. mushrooms
2 oz. tomato
chopped parsley for garnish

Cut the veal into cubes and place it in a saucepan
with the chicken stock, tomato juice, onion
flakes, salt, pepper, garlic powder and paprika
pepper. Bring to the boil, cover and simmer
for 15 minutes.
Wash the mushrooms and slice. Put the tomato
in boiling water for 1 minute. Rinse in cold
water and then remove the skin and chop.
Add the mushrooms and tomato to the saucepan
and continue cooking for a further 20 minutes.
Serve sprinkled with chopped parsley.

WIENER SCHNITZEL — Lunch

Serves Two

4×3 oz. veal escalopes
juice of 1 lemon
salt and pepper
2 fl. oz. skimmed milk
2 oz. fresh white breadcrumbs
lemon slices, cauliflower sprigs and chopped
parsley for garnish

Beat the escalopes between two pieces of
greaseproof paper until very thin. Place them in
a shallow dish to marinate in lemon juice for
one hour. Dip the escalopes in seasoned milk,
then into the breadcrumbs. Cook the escalopes
in a non-stick frying pan for about 20 minutes
until golden brown on both sides. Serve on a
hot dish garnished with lemon slices, raw
cauliflower sprigs and chopped parsley.

SPICY CASSEROLE — Dinner

Serves Three

1 lb. 2oz. cooked lamb
2 teaspoons dry mustard
8 fl. oz. chicken stock made with chicken stock cube
   and water
½ teaspoon dried mixed herbs
1 medium-sized cooking apple
1 lemon
1 orange
4 drops artificial liquid sweetener
½ teaspoon paprika pepper

Cut the lamb into 1 inch cubes. Place the meat
in a shallow casserole. Stir the mustard into
stock, add the herbs and pour over meat.
Peel, core and slice the apple into thickish rings
and place them on top of the meat. Sprinkle
with the grated rinds and juice of the lemon and
orange with the artificial sweetener. Sprinkle
with paprika pepper. Cover and bake in the
centre of a moderately hot oven (375°F. Mark 5)
for about 35 minutes.

LAMB KEBABS — Dinner

Serves One

8 oz. lamb fillet
6 small tomatoes
2 oz. button mushrooms
½ green pepper
cauliflower sprigs and watercress for garnish

Marinade:
2 fl. oz. wine vinegar
1 clove garlic
1 sprig rosemary
pinch of dried basil
salt and pepper

Cut the lamb into 1 inch cubes. Place them in a
bowl. Combine the ingredients for marinade
and pour them over the meat. Cover and leave
overnight.
Next day, place the lamb, tomatoes, mushrooms
and pepper, cut into squares, alternately on
skewers. Season. Cook under a moderately hot
grill for about 20 minutes, turning constantly,
basting occasionally with the marinade. Place
the kebabs on a serving plate and garnish with
watercress and cauliflower sprigs.

Veal Marengo (opposite)   *Moussaka (above)*

LAMB PROVENÇALE   Dinner

Serves Four

1 × 2½ lb. leg of lamb
2 cloves garlic, crushed
salt
2 tablespoons wine vinegar
1¾ pints chicken stock made with water and chicken
  stock cube
ground black pepper
8 oz. canned carrots
8 oz. canned petit pois
1 lb. button mushrooms
watercress for garnishing

Wipe the lamb and spread the crushed garlic and salt over the surface. Fry the meat gently in a flameproof casserole on all sides for about 10–15 minutes. Add the vinegar, bring to the boil and cook rapidly until reduced. Pour over 1 pint of the stock and season with plenty of black pepper. Cover and bake in the centre of a moderate oven (350°F. Mark 4) for about 1¼–1½ hours.
Transfer the lamb to a serving plate and keep warm. Pour away the liquid in the casserole. Add the drained vegetables together with the ½ pint of stock, and heat through. Cook the sliced mushrooms in the remaining ¼ pint stock in a saucepan. Drain the vegetables and spoon these around the meat. Serve garnished with watercress.

71

MOUSSAKA — Dinner

Serves One

6 fl. oz. tomato juice
1 tablespoon dried onion flakes
2 oz. mushrooms
4 oz. cooked peas or diced carrot
1 stick cooked celery, chopped
1 teaspoon dried parsley
celery salt
garlic powder
salt and pepper
6 oz. minced cooked beef, veal or lamb
4 oz. aubergine

Place the tomato juice in a saucepan with the onion flakes. Wash and chop the mushrooms and add to the pan. Bring to the boil, simmer for 5 minutes. Add the cooked vegetables, parsley and seasonings to taste. Continue cooking until boiling again.
Slice the aubergine thinly and place in a colander in layers, sprinkling each layer with salt liberally. Put a plate on top and put aside for 1 hour. Drain off any liquid.
Place the minced cooked meat in an ovenproof dish, add the vegetable mixture and mix thoroughly. Arrange the aubergine slices on top. Bake in a moderate oven (350°F. Mark 4) for 30–40 minutes or until the aubergine is lightly browned.

SPAGHETTI BOLOGNAISE — Lunch

Serves Two

12 oz. tomato juice
¼ teaspoon dried oregano
1 bay leaf
¼ teaspoon garlic salt
artificial sweetener to equal 1 tablespoon sugar
8 oz. minced cooked beef or lamb
6 oz. cooked spaghetti
parsley for garnish

Place the tomato juice in a saucepan with the oregano, bay leaf, garlic salt, artificial sweetener and minced meat. Bring to the boil, cover and simmer for 25 minutes. Remove and discard the bay leaf.
Arrange the hot, freshly cooked spaghetti on a serving plate. Pour the Bolognaise sauce over the spaghetti and serve garnished with a sprig of parsley.

SHEPHERD'S PIE — Dinner

Serves One

6 oz. minced lean cooked lamb
¼ pint tomato juice
4 tablespoons beef stock made with beef stock cube and water
1½ teaspoons dried onion flakes
1½ teaspoons dried pepper flakes
1½ teaspoons dried celery flakes
salt and pepper to taste
1 teaspoon dried mixed herbs
3 oz. cooked potato
paprika pepper

Place the lamb in a saucepan with the tomato juice, stock, dried vegetable flakes, salt and pepper and mixed herbs. Bring to the boil, stirring, cover pan and simmer for 15 minutes. Spoon the meat mixture into an ovenproof dish. Mash the cooked potato and place on top of the meat. Sprinkle with a little paprika pepper. Reheat in a hot oven (400°F. Mark 6) for 15 minutes.

RABBIT WITH PEPPERS — Dinner

Serves Two

1 lb. boned rabbit
salt and black pepper
4 oz. onion
2 tomatoes
1½ pints chicken stock made with water and chicken stock cubes
1 teaspoon dried rosemary
1 clove garlic, crushed
2 green peppers
3 tablespoons chopped parsley for garnishing

Wash and dry the rabbit, cut into serving portions, season and place in a non-stick saucepan. Brown lightly. Slice the onion, cook the tomato in boiling water for 1 minute, skin and chop roughly. Add the stock to the saucepan with the tomato, rosemary and garlic. Cover the pan and simmer for about 50 minutes. Remove the seeds and membranes from the peppers, slice and add to the pan for for the last 10 minutes of the cooking time. Place the rabbit on a hot serving plate and spoon over the drained onion, tomato and pepper mixture. Garnish with chopped parsley.

LIVER AND APPLE CASSEROLE Dinner

Serves One

1 teaspoon dried onion flakes
1 medium cooking apple
8 oz. lamb's liver
salt and pepper
½ pint tomato juice
4 oz. tomato
3 oz. cooked rice

Sprinkle the onion flakes in the base of an
ovenproof casserole. Slice the apple and arrange
half of the slices on the onion. Slice the liver.
Season and place it on the apple. Top with the
remaining apple slices and pour the tomato
juice into the casserole. Cover and bake in a
moderate oven (350°F. Mark 4) for 30 minutes.
Slice the tomato and arrange it on the top of the
casserole. Return the casserole to the oven and
cook, uncovered, for a further 5 minutes.
Drain off liquid before serving with the hot
freshly cooked rice.

HONG KONG LIVER BARBECUE

Dinner

Serves Two

1 lb. lamb's liver
6 tablespoons soy sauce
½ teaspoon Aromat
2 slivers fresh root ginger
artificial sweetener to equal 2 teaspoons sugar
6 oz. cooked rice

Slice the liver and place in a shallow dish.
Mix together the soy sauce, Aromat, ginger and
artificial sweetener. Pour the mixture over the
liver and marinate in a cool place for 4–6 hours.
Drain the liver.
Cook the liver under a moderately hot grill for
about 15 minutes, turning frequently.
Arrange the hot, freshly cooked rice on a
serving plate and place the cooked liver on top.

LIVER KEBABS Dinner

Serves One

8 oz. lamb's liver
1 tablespoon wine or malt vinegar
3 tablespoons tomato juice
salt and pepper
2 oz. onions
2 oz. tomato
2 oz. mushrooms
2 oz. green peppers
3 oz. cooked rice
green salad for serving

Cut the liver into cubes. Mix the vinegar with
the tomato juice and season well. Marinate the
liver in this mixture for at least 2 hours.
Cut the vegetables into bite-sized pieces and
arrange them, with the liver, on skewers.
Place under a moderately hot grill and cook for
about 20 minutes, basting occasionally with the
marinade. Turn the kebabs once.
Arrange the hot, freshly cooked rice on a
serving plate and place the kebabs on top.
Serve a green salad separately.

LAMB'S LIVER CASSEROLE Lunch

Serves Two

12 oz. lamb's liver
1 chilli
4 oz. mushrooms
1 stick celery
1 tablespoon dried onion flakes
1 clove garlic
½ pint beef stock made with beef stock cube and water
¼ teaspoon salt
black pepper
2 tablespoons cider vinegar

Wipe the liver and cut into thin slices. De-seed
and chop the chilli, slice the mushrooms and
celery. Soak the onion flakes. Place the liver in
alternate layers with the vegetables in a casserole.
Add the clove of garlic and stock. Season with
salt and pepper. Cover and bake in a moderately
slow oven (325°F. Mark 3) for about 45 minutes.
15 minutes before cooking time is finished, take
out the clove of garlic and add the cider
vinegar. Drain off the cooking liquid. Serve hot.

KIDNEYS IN TOMATO SAUCE   Dinner

Serves Two

1 lb. lamb's kidneys
½ pint chicken stock made with chicken stock cube and
   water
peas for serving

Sauce:
12 fl. oz. tomato juice
1 tablespoon wine vinegar
2 teaspoons dry mustard
¼ teaspoon salt
black pepper

Skin and core the kidneys. Simmer them in the chicken stock in a saucepan until tender for about 40 minutes. Drain.
Combine the tomato juice, vinegar and mustard together in a small saucepan. Season with salt and pepper. Bring the sauce to the boil.
Place the kidneys on a serving dish and pour the sauce over. Serve with peas.

HUNGARIAN KIDNEYS   Lunch

Serves One

4 oz. cooked ox kidney
1 tablespoon dried onion flakes
beef stock made with beef stock cube and water
¼ small cabbage
1 tablespoon pickled red cabbage
2 oz. button mushrooms
1 oz. breadcrumbs
pinch of ground ginger
salt and pepper to taste

Skin the kidney, remove the core and chop roughly. Put into a saucepan with the onion flakes and enough stock to just cover. Bring to the boil. Cover and simmer for about 15 minutes.
Meanwhile, shred the cabbage and cook in a saucepan of boiling salted water until just tender. Drain well. Stir in the red cabbage. Keep hot.
Slice the mushrooms and add them to the kidneys with the breadcrumbs, ginger, salt and pepper. Continue cooking for a further 5 minutes.
Arrange the cabbage in a ring on a heated serving plate. Spoon the kidney mixture into the centre of the cabbage.

GERMAN LIVER SAUSAGE   Lunch

Serves Two

8 oz. cooked liver
1 teaspoon dried onion flakes
1 teaspoon caraway seeds
1 clove garlic, crushed
2 tablespoons red wine vinegar
salt and pepper to taste
green salad for serving

Chop the liver coarsely and place in a small saucepan with about 3 tablespoons water, the onion flakes, caraway seeds and garlic. Cook gently, stirring occasionally, for 10 minutes. Drain off any remaining liquid.
Mince the liver mixture finely, putting it through the mincer twice if necessary. Add the vinegar, salt and pepper and beat well with a wooden spoon to make a firm paste. Place on a piece of foil and shape to form a sausage or loaf. Seal the ends and place the sausage in the refrigerator to become firm.
Arrange a green salad on a serving plate, slice the liver sausage and place it on the salad.

HERBED TRIPE   Lunch

Serves Four

12 oz. tripe
½ pint tomato juice
1 teaspoon dried mixed herbs or marjoram
4 oz. grated Cheddar cheese

Cut the tripe into squares. Place in a saucepan with salted water to cover and simmer for 30 minutes. Drain. Place the tripe in a saucepan with the tomato juice and herbs and simmer for a further 1 hour. Drain off the liquid.
Place the tripe on a hot serving dish. Top with the grated cheese and serve immediately.

German Liver Sausage (opposite top)
Hungarian Kidneys (opposite bottom)

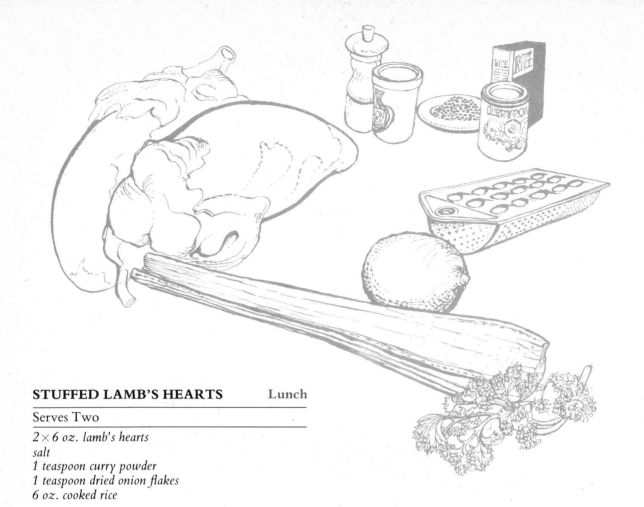

STUFFED LAMB'S HEARTS — Lunch

Serves Two

2 × 6 oz. lamb's hearts
salt
1 teaspoon curry powder
1 teaspoon dried onion flakes
6 oz. cooked rice

Stuffing:
2 oz. wholemeal breadcrumbs
1 tablespoon chopped parsley
1 stick celery, finely chopped
grated rind of 1 lemon
salt and pepper
chicken stock made from chicken stock cube and
    water

Trim the hearts and remove the sinews and fat
with a pair of scissors. Snip through the centre
division to make one cavity in each heart.
Soak in salted cold water to cover, for 1 hour.
Make the stuffing by mixing all the ingredients
together thoroughly, using just enough chicken
stock to bind.
Stuff the prepared hearts and close the opening
with wooden cocktail sticks. Place them in a
shallow ovenproof dish and add ½ pint water,
the curry powder and dried onion flakes. Cover
the dish and cook in a slow oven (300°F. Mark 2)
for 2½ hours or until tender. Baste hearts
occasionally during the cooking. Drain off
liquid before serving.
Arrange the hot, freshly cooked rice on a
serving plate. Slice the cooked hearts and place
on the rice.

WHITE CABBAGE SOUP WITH MEATBALLS — Dinner

Serves Two

1 small white cabbage
2 pints chicken stock made with chicken stock cube
    and water
freshly ground black pepper
pinch of ground allspice
few drops artificial liquid sweetener

Meatballs:
12 oz. minced cooked veal or chicken
2 oz. breadcrumbs
1 teaspoon dried onion flakes
salt and pepper

Shred the cabbage finely and place it in a
saucepan with the stock, pepper, allspice and
sweetener. Bring to the boil, stirring, cover pan
and simmer for 20–25 minutes.
Put the minced veal or chicken into a bowl,
mix in the breadcrumbs, onion flakes, salt and
pepper and a little water to bind. Form into 6
balls. Carefully drop the balls into the soup and
cook for 5 minutes.

POULTRY

Whether it is a turkey for Christmas or a chicken for Saturday supper in the kitchen, poultry needs careful cooking if the recipes are to be a success. Both turkey and chicken soon become dry if cooked for too long, especially when roasting. The best method of roasting is in foil because that keeps the flesh moist. Place the oven-ready bird on a large sheet of foil, sprinkle with seasoning and herbs (tarragon is especially good with chicken), wrap foil completely over the bird, place in a baking dish and roast in the usual way. With poultry, as with all other foods, make a point of serving up attractively. A few rings of red or green pepper, or some sprigs of parsley or watercress, do wonders for a dull looking dish.

TOMATO CHICKEN BAKE   Dinner

Serves Four

4 tablespoons dried onion flakes
4 oz. button mushrooms
2 tablespoons chopped celery
4 oz. canned peppers
1 clove garlic, crushed
good pinch of dried rosemary
pinch of ground allspice
14 fl. oz. tomato juice
1 tablespoon lemon juice
4 × 10 oz. chicken joints
salt and freshly ground black pepper
watercress for garnish

Put the onion flakes into a saucepan with the washed and sliced mushrooms, celery, 2 tablespoons chopped canned peppers, garlic, rosemary, allspice and tomato juice. Bring to the boil, stirring occasionally and then simmer, uncovered, until the tomato juice is reduced by half. Stir in the lemon juice.
Cut each chicken joint in half, remove the skin and sprinkle with salt and pepper. Heat a non-stick frying pan and brown the chicken gently, turning frequently.
Place the chicken in an ovenproof casserole. Spoon some of the tomato sauce over each portion. Bake in a moderately slow oven (325°F. Mark 3) for 35 minutes or until the chicken is tender. Baste with the tomato sauce every 10 minutes during cooking.
Serve, garnished with sprigs of watercress and the remaining canned peppers cut into thin strips.

CHICKEN CURRY   Lunch

Serves One

4 oz. cooked chicken
2 oz. mushrooms
$\frac{1}{4}$ pint tomato juice
$\frac{1}{2}$ teaspoon Worcestershire sauce
$\frac{1}{8}$ teaspoon garlic salt
2–3 teaspoons curry powder (according to taste)
$\frac{1}{2}$ green pepper
$\frac{1}{4}$ teaspoon salt
$\frac{1}{2}$ red-skinned apple
3 oz. cooked rice

Chop the chicken roughly. Slice the mushrooms and place them in a saucepan with the tomato juice and chicken. Add the Worcestershire sauce, garlic salt and curry powder. Bring to the boil and simmer for 15 minutes.
Remove seeds and membranes from the pepper. Cook in a small saucepan of boiling salted water for 3–5 minutes. Remove and drain. Chop the apple and the pepper and add to the curry. Simmer for a further 5 minutes. Arrange the hot, freshly cooked rice on a serving plate and spoon the curry on top.

CHICKEN SPECIAL   Dinner

Serves Four

4 × 10 oz. chicken joints
salt and pepper
8 oz. button mushrooms
2 sticks celery
3 tablespoons dried onion flakes
2 sprigs parsley
2 bay leaves
2 cloves garlic, crushed
$\frac{3}{4}$ pint chicken stock made with water and chicken stock cube
chopped parsley
12 oz. cooked rice and green salad for serving

Divide each chicken joint into two. Remove the skin and season with salt and pepper. Heat a non-stick frying pan and cook the chicken until browned all over. Place chicken in an ovenproof dish. Cover and bake in a moderate oven (350°F. Mark 4) for 35 minutes.
Wash the mushrooms and slice thinly. Slice the celery. Place the mushrooms and celery in a saucepan with the onion flakes, parsley sprigs, bay leaves, garlic and stock. Bring to the boil, stirring, and then cover and simmer for 30 minutes. Remove and discard the parsley and bay leaves. Return to the boil and boil rapidly until the liquid is reduced by half. Adjust seasoning.
Drain the cooked chicken joints and place in a serving dish. Pour the vegetable sauce over the top and garnish with chopped parsley.
Serve with the hot freshly cooked rice and a green salad.

Tomato Chicken Bake (opposite)

CHICKEN PATTIES

Serves One

2 oz. mushrooms
2 teaspoons dried onion flakes
4 tablespoons skimmed milk
4 oz. minced cooked chicken
1 oz. white breadcrumbs
salt and pepper
pinch of ground nutmeg
$\frac{1}{2}$ teaspoon skimmed milk powder
3 oz. cooked rice

Chop the mushrooms finely and put into a
small saucepan with the onion flakes and the
milk. Bring to the boil and simmer very gently
for about 5 minutes.
Mix the chicken with the breadcrumbs, salt,
pepper and nutmeg in a bowl. Add the
mushroom mixture and combine, adding a
little extra milk if necessary to bind the mixture
together.
Shape the mixture into 4 flat patties. Sprinkle
with the milk powder and grill under a
moderately hot grill for about 5 minutes,
turning once.
Arrange the hot, freshly cooked rice on a
serving plate and place the chicken patties on top.

CHICKEN VEGETABLE RISOTTO

Serves Two

2 oz. onion
1 pint chicken stock made from chicken stock cube
    and water
4 oz. mushrooms
1 small cauliflower
4 oz. cooked chicken
4 oz. cooked carrot
2 oz. cooked peas
6 oz. cooked rice
2 oz. grated Parmesan cheese

Chop the onion and place in a non-stick
saucepan with enough of the stock to moisten.
Cook gently, stirring constantly, until browned.
Wash and slice the mushrooms and add to the
pan with the cauliflower, broken into flowerettes,
and the remaining stock. Bring to the boil and
simmer until the cauliflower is tender.
Add the chicken, cooked vegetables and cooked
rice. Reheat gently, stirring constantly.
Pile on to a heated serving plate and sprinkle
the cheese over the top.

SPICY CHICKEN

Serves One

4 oz. onion
2 large tomatoes
1 stick celery
1 oz. button mushrooms
$\frac{1}{4}$ green pepper
2 slices white cabbage
few sprigs of cauliflower
1 tablespoon soy sauce
3 tablespoons water
garlic salt
black pepper
6 oz. cooked chicken
3 tablespoons bean sprouts
tomato slices and watercress for garnishing

Slice the onion. Place the tomatoes in boiling
water for 1 minute. Skin and cut in quarters.
Chop the celery. Wash the mushrooms and
remove the stalks. Remove the seeds and
membranes from the pepper and slice thinly.
Shred the cabbage. Place the prepared
vegetables in a saucepan. Add the soy sauce,
water, garlic salt and pepper. Cover the pan and
cook gently until tender. Cut the chicken into
bite-sized pieces and add to the saucepan, with
the bean sprouts, and heat gently for about
25 minutes.
Place on a hot serving plate and garnish with
tomato slices and watercress.

CHICKEN WITH GOOSEBERRIES
Dinner

Serves Four

1 × 2½ lb. boiling chicken
4 oz. carrot
4 oz. onion
4 oz. celery
4 oz. mushrooms
1 tablespoon chopped parsley
salt and pepper
1 pint chicken stock made with chicken stock cube
    and water
12 oz. gooseberries
low calorie orange squash
artificial sweetener

Place the chicken in a large saucepan with cold
salted water to cover. Bring to the boil and
simmer, covered, for 2–3 hours or until tender.
Meanwhile, slice the vegetables thinly. Place the
carrot, onion and celery in a saucepan with the
chopped parsley, salt and pepper and chicken
stock. Bring to the boil, cover and simmer until
the vegetables are almost tender. Add the
mushrooms and continue cooking until all the
vegetables are cooked.
Top and tail the gooseberries and cook in a
saucepan with low calorie orange squash to
almost cover, until soft. Add a little sweetener
if required.
Skin the chicken and cut into 4 portions.
Arrange the chicken on a serving plate and place
the drained vegetables and the drained
gooseberries around it.

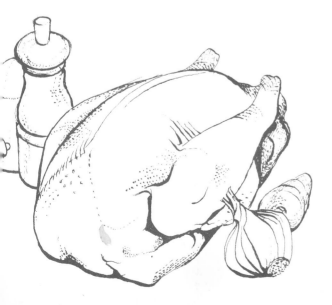

CURRIED CHICKEN OMELETTE Lunch

Serves Four

4 oz. onion
½ teaspoon ground turmeric
2 cloves garlic, crushed
2 green chillies, chopped
½ teaspoon ground ginger
8 oz. cooked chicken
4 tablespoons water
salt and black pepper
4 eggs
2 tablespoons water
tomato wedges for garnish
green salad for serving

Slice the onions and brown them in a non-stick
saucepan. Add the turmeric, garlic, chopped
chillies and ginger. Cook, stirring, for 5
minutes. Add the chicken and water and cook
for a further 3 minutes. Season well.
Beat the eggs, water and seasoning together in a
bowl. Make an omelette in a non-stick frying
pan. When the omelette is almost cooked put
filling on top and fold over.
Place the omelette on a hot serving dish and
garnish with tomato wedges. Serve with a
green salad.

DEVILLED GRILLED CHICKEN   Lunch

Serves Two

12 oz. skinned chicken breasts
2 oz. fresh white breadcrumbs
salt and freshly ground black pepper
¼ teaspoon dried thyme
¼ teaspoon garlic powder
good pinch of cayenne pepper
2 tablespoons French mustard
2 tablespoons skimmed milk
lemon wedges and watercress for garnish

Prepare the chicken breasts. Place the
breadcrumbs in a shallow dish.
Place the salt and pepper, thyme, garlic powder,
cayenne pepper, mustard and milk into a bowl
and mix thoroughly.
Coat the chicken breasts all over with the
devilled mixture and then dip into the
breadcrumbs, pressing them on firmly. Place
the chicken in a grill pan and cook under a
moderate grill for about 15–20 minutes each
side, or until the chicken is cooked and the
crumbs are golden.
Serve garnished with lemon wedges and
watercress.

Weight Watchers Coq-au-Vin (above)

Paella (opposite)

WEIGHT WATCHERS COQ-AU-VIN

Dinner

Serves Four

4 × 10 oz. chicken portions
8 oz. button onions
1¼ pints chicken stock made with chicken stock cube
  and water
¼ pint red wine vinegar
bouquet garni
8 oz. button mushrooms
peas for serving

Marinade:
2 tablespoons dried onion flakes
salt and freshly ground black pepper
1 clove garlic, crushed
½ pint tomato juice
¼ pint red wine vinegar
½ pint chicken stock made with chicken stock cube
  and water

Skin the chicken joints and place in a shallow dish. Mix all the ingredients for the marinade together in a bowl and pour them over the chicken. Marinate for about 6 hours, in a cool place.
Drain the chicken—reserve the marinade. Heat a non-stick frying pan and cook the chicken until golden all over. Remove the chicken and place in casserole. Brown the onions in the frying pan and then add them to the casserole with the chicken stock, vinegar and bouquet garni. Cook in a moderate oven (350°F. Mark 4) for 1 hour. Wash the mushrooms and add them to the casserole 20 minutes before the cooking time is completed. Meanwhile, pour the reserved marinade into a saucepan. Bring to the boil and boil briskly for 5–10 minutes or until reduced slightly.
Drain the chicken, mushrooms and onions and place in a serving dish. Pour the hot sauce over the top.
Serve the peas separately.

PAELLA Dinner

Serves Four

12 oz. cooked chicken
8 oz. onion
1 clove garlic, crushed
1 pint chicken stock made with chicken stock cube and
  water
12 oz. cooked rice
2 tomatoes
4 oz. lobster
4 oz. cooked mussels
4 oz. prawns
8 oz. cooked peas
1 red pepper

Cut the chicken into bite-sized pieces, chop the
onion. Place the chicken and onion in a pan with
the garlic and stock. Bring to the boil and
simmer for 15 minutes. Stir in the cooked rice.
Plunge the tomatoes in boiling water for
1 minute. Rinse in cold water, skin and chop.
Add to the pan. Arrange the lobster, mussels,
prawns, peas and sliced pepper on the top.
Continue cooking, very gently, until the liquid
is all absorbed—about 15 minutes.
Serve in the cooking pan.

SWEET SOUR CHICKEN Dinner

Serves One

1×10 oz. portion chicken
1 tablespoon lemon juice
1 tablespoon soy sauce
3 tablespoons water
artificial sweetener to taste
2 oz. mushrooms
3 oz. cooked egg noodles

Skin the chicken and place in an ovenproof
dish. Mix together the lemon juice, soy sauce,
water and artificial sweetener and pour over the
chicken. Cover the dish. Place the chicken in a
cool place to marinate for 2 hours. Cook
covered, in a moderately slow oven (325°F.
Mark 3) for $1\frac{1}{4}$ hours.
Wash and slice the mushrooms. Uncover the
chicken and arrange the mushrooms on top.
Cook for a further 15 minutes, basting
frequently.
Arrange the hot, freshly cooked noodles on a
serving plate and place chicken on top.

CHICKEN LIVER MOUSSE Lunch

Serves Two

8 oz. button mushrooms
$\frac{1}{4}$ pint chicken stock made with chicken stock cube and
  water
2 tablespoons skimmed milk powder
salt and black pepper
$\frac{1}{2}$ oz. gelatine
2 tablespoons cold water
8 oz. cooked chicken livers
$\frac{1}{4}$ pint tomato juice
1 teaspoon Worcestershire sauce
green salad for serving

Chop the mushrooms finely and simmer for
10 minutes in a saucepan with the chicken stock.
Stir in the milk powder, salt and black pepper
to taste. Dissolve the gelatine in the water over a
pan of hot water and stir into the mushroom
sauce. Mince the cooked livers and stir into the
mushroom sauce, with the tomato juice and
Worcestershire sauce. Taste and adjust the
seasoning. Pour into a wetted $1\frac{1}{2}$ pint ring mould.
When set, unmould on to a serving plate and
serve with a green salad.

CHICKEN TIMBALES Lunch

Serves One

4 oz. cooked chicken
1 tablespoon finely chopped green pepper
1 tablespoon finely chopped red pepper
1 tablespoon dried onion flakes
1 tablespoon lemon juice
salt and black pepper
1 tablespoon mayonnaise
3 fl. oz. skimmed milk
2 teaspoons gelatine
$\frac{1}{4}$ pint water
watercress, lemon twists and sliced tomato for
  garnishing

Chop the chicken and mix it with the peppers,
soaked onion flakes, lemon juice and seasoning.
Add the mayonnaise and skimmed milk.
Dissolve the gelatine in water over a pan of hot
water and allow to cool. Add the gelatine to
the mixture and place in a wetted 1 pint
ring mould.
Chill until set and unmould on a serving plate.
Garnish with watercress, lemon twists and
slices of tomato.

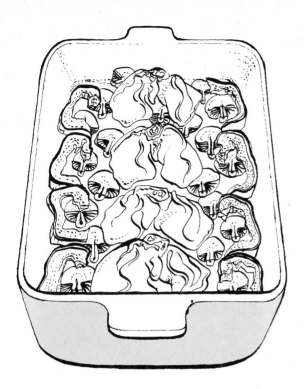

SAVOURY CHICKEN LIVERS WITH MUSHROOMS Dinner

Serves Two

16 oz. chicken livers
8 oz. mushrooms
1 tablespoon dried onion flakes
¾ pint chicken stock made with chicken stock cube
    and water
4 tablespoons skimmed milk powder
½ teaspoon curry powder
1 bay leaf
1 green pepper
pinch of dried oregano
salt and pepper

Cook the chicken livers in a saucepan with
water to cover until tender. Drain. Wash and
slice the mushrooms. Stir the onion flakes into
the chicken stock and allow them to soften.
Stir in the milk powder and curry powder.
Spread the mushrooms over the base of an
ovenproof dish. Remove the seeds and
membranes from the pepper, slice thinly and
arrange on top of the mushrooms. Place the
chicken livers evenly on the pepper. Add the bay
leaf and oregano to the sauce, adjust the
seasoning and pour over the chicken livers.
Bake in a hot oven (400°F. Mark 6) for
20–25 minutes.

CHEESY CHICKEN AND ASPARAGUS SALAD Lunch

Serves Four

1 × 12 oz. can asparagus tips
12 oz. cooked chicken
1 red-skinned apple
juice of ½ lemon
4 oz. cottage cheese
4 tablespoons mayonnaise
salt and freshly ground black pepper
mustard and cress
lettuce
parsley and strips of pepper for garnish

Drain the asparagus, reserve a few for garnishing,
chop the remainder. Dice the chicken. Dice the
apple and mix with the lemon juice. Place the
chopped asparagus in a bowl with the chicken,
apple, cottage cheese, mayonnaise, salt and black
pepper to taste. Add a little mustard and cress
and combine thoroughly.
Arrange the lettuce in a serving dish. Pile the
chicken mixture on top. Garnish with the
reserved asparagus tips, sprigs of parsley and
strips of red pepper.

STUFFED TURKEY Dinner

Serves Eight

1 × 5½–6 lb. oven-ready turkey
1 teaspoon dried sage
3 teaspoons dried onion flakes
1 × 7½ oz. can mushrooms
salt and black pepper
3 tablespoons chicken stock made with chicken stock
    cube and water
watercress for garnish

Wipe the turkey and place it in a roasting pan.
Combine the sage, soaked onion flakes,
mushrooms, salt and black pepper. Bind
together with the chicken stock. Stuff the body
cavity with the stuffing. Cover with foil and
cook in the centre of a moderate oven
(350°F. Mark 4) for about 2 hours.
Transfer to a hot serving dish and serve
garnished with watercress, accompanied with
Brussels sprouts and bread sauce.

Cheesy Chicken and Asparagus Salad (above)

JELLIED CHICKEN

Serves Four

8 oz. button mushrooms
1 tablespoon lemon juice
black pepper
1 lb. cooked chicken
1 oz. gelatine
3 tablespoons water
1½ pints chicken stock made with chicken stock cubes
   and water
½ red pepper
2 tablespoons chopped parsley
8 oz. cooked diced carrots
8 oz. cooked peas

Wash the mushrooms and remove the stalks and slice. Place them in a small saucepan and simmer for 2 minutes in lemon juice and black pepper. Leave to cool. Cut the chicken into small cubes. Dissolve the gelatine in the water over a pan of hot water. Pour into the chicken stock with the strained lemon juice from the mushrooms. Remove the seeds and membranes from the pepper, slice and arrange the slices with the chopped parsley in the base of a wet 2 pint ring mould. Pour over a little of the stock and leave to set in a cold place. When set,

arrange the chicken and mushrooms in the mould and when the stock is syrupy and almost set, pour it over the chicken. Leave to set in a cold place.
To serve, unmould on to a serving plate. Fill the centre with the cooked, mixed vegetables.

VIENNESE BRAWN

Serves Four

8 oz. cooked chicken
4 hard-boiled eggs
3 teaspoons gelatine
2 tablespoons cold water
¾ pint chicken stock made with chicken stock cube
   and water
watercress and asparagus tips for garnishing

Dice the cooked chicken. Rinse a 1½ pint ring mould with cold water and arrange slices of hard-boiled eggs on the base and sides of the mould. Add the cooked chicken. Dissolve the gelatine in the water over a pan of hot water and then stir it into the stock and put in a cold place until on the point of setting. Pour over chicken and egg. Leave to set in a cold place.
To serve, unmould on to a serving dish and garnish with watercress and asparagus tips.

VEGETABLES AND SALADS

Vegetables and salads play an important part in the daily eating routine of anyone who wants to be healthy and slim. The advantage of many vegetables is that their visual appeal is far greater than their fattening power. If you simply must have a nibble, you won't come to very much harm if you vent your hungry feelings on a handful of crispy, crunchy radishes, or raw button mushrooms which have been washed and dried and sprinkled with garlic salt.

Vegetables and salads, fruits, too, should be bought as fresh as possible to ensure the best flavour and to make them thoroughly appetizing. Treat yourself to the best-looking tomatoes, the fattest asparagus. You can afford them now that you are not buying fattening, extravagant luxuries. Keep a 'nibble' bowl in the refrigerator made up of crunchy raw vegetables like cauliflower, green pepper, celery, radishes, cabbages and cucumber, cleaned, chopped and crisped and all ready to eat. When an emergency does arrive, and your hand automatically stretches out for something to eat, the nibble bowl is there to save you.

BAKED AUBERGINES

Serves Four

1–2 aubergines (1 lb. weight)
2 teaspoons dried onion flakes
1 teaspoon mixed herbs
salt and pepper
4 tablespoons vegetable oil

Wash the aubergines and wrap in foil. Bake in a moderate oven (350°F. Mark 4) for 30 minutes to 1 hour, depending on the size, until tender. Cut the cooked aubergines in half lengthwise and scoop out the flesh. Put the pulp in a bowl and mix with the onion flakes, mixed herbs, salt, pepper and oil. Return to the aubergine skins. Place the stuffed aubergines in an oven-proof dish. Return to the oven and reheat for a few minutes.

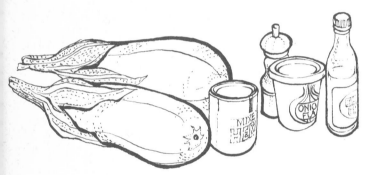

STUFFED AUBERGINES

Serves Four

2 aubergines (to weigh 1 lb.)
2 tomatoes
1 tablespoon dried onion flakes
1 green pepper
salt and pepper to taste
3 fl. oz. tomato juice
4 tablespoons vegetable oil

Place the aubergines in a large saucepan of boiling water and cook for 5 minutes. Drain. Cut in halves lengthwise and carefully scoop out the flesh and chop. Reserve the skins. Immerse the tomatoes in boiling water for 1 minute, rinse in cold water and skin. Soak the onion flakes until softened. Remove the seeds and membranes from the pepper. Chop the tomatoes and pepper. Mix all the prepared vegetables together in a saucepan and season to taste. Add the tomato juice, bring to the boil, stirring occasionally, simmer for 10 minutes. Place the aubergine skins in a shallow ovenproof dish and fill them with the vegetable mixture. Bake in a moderate oven (350°F. Mark 4) for 30–40 minutes.
Pour 1 tablespoon of oil over each aubergine half and serve as soon as possible.

BAVARIAN CABBAGE

Serves One

½ white cabbage
4 oz. onion
2 tablespoons vinegar
½ teaspoon caraway seeds
salt
few drops artificial liquid sweetener

Shred the cabbage finely. Chop the onion finely. Place the cabbage and onion in a saucepan with ½ pint water, vinegar, caraway seeds and salt. Cover the pan and cook over a low heat, shaking the pan gently occasionally, for 30 minutes or until the cabbage is tender. Drain. Stir in the sweetener and serve.

HOT RED CABBAGE WITH APPLE

Serves One

6 oz. red cabbage
1 oz. dried onion flakes
1 medium-sized cooking apple
salt
1 tablespoon wine vinegar
3 drops artificial liquid sweetener

Chop the red cabbage finely. Soak the onion flakes until softened. Peel and slice the apple. Heat a non-stick saucepan, add the drained onion and fry until browned. Add ¼ pint cold water, the cabbage and the apple with salt to taste. Bring to the boil, cover the pan and simmer gently until the cabbage is tender, adding more water if required.
Drain off all the liquid and stir in the vinegar and sweetener. Cook very gently for a further 3–4 minutes.

HERBED MUSHROOMS

Serves Two to Three

1 lb. mushrooms
2 chicken stock cubes
salt and freshly ground black pepper
1 teaspoon dried oregano or marjoram

Wash the mushrooms and slice thinly. Put them into a large non-stick frying pan with the crumbled stock cubes, seasonings and oregano. Add enough water to cover. Cover the frying pan, bring to the boil and simmer for about 10 minutes. Drain.
Serve hot.

STUFFED ONIONS

Serves Four

4 × 4 oz. onions
2 oz. mushrooms
½ teaspoon dried mixed herbs
2 tablespoons skimmed milk
salt and pepper

Peel the onions, slice off the tops and hollow out about ½ of the centre of each.
Chop the onion pieces. Wash and chop the mushrooms and mix with the chopped onion, herbs, milk, salt and pepper. Stand the hollowed out onions in a shallow ovenproof dish, fill them with the stuffing. Put any left over in the base of the dish. Cover with foil and bake in a hot oven (400°F. Mark 6) for about 1¼ hours.
Serve with roast beef or beefburgers.

SPICY BAKED TOMATOES

Serves Four

8 medium-sized tomatoes (1 lb. weight)
1 tablespoon made mustard
1 tablespoon dried onion flakes
2 tablespoons chopped green pepper
2 tablespoons chopped celery
½ teaspoon salt
4 tablespoons skimmed milk

Cut the tomatoes in half and place them, cut side up, in a shallow ovenproof dish. Spread each half with mustard. Mix the onion flakes with the pepper, celery and salt, sprinkle over the tomatoes. Spoon the milk gently over each tomato half. Bake the tomatoes in a hot oven (400°F. Mark 6) for about 15 minutes.

WEIGHT WATCHERS RATATOUILLE

Serves Four

½ pint tomato juice
1 chicken stock cube
2 teaspoons dried onion flakes
2 teaspoons dried pepper flakes
2 tablespoons wine vinegar
artificial liquid sweetener to equal 4 teaspoons sugar
salt and pepper
1 small marrow
4 tablespoons vegetable oil

Put the tomato juice in a saucepan with the stock cube, onion flakes, pepper flakes, vinegar, artificial sweetener, salt and pepper. Bring to the boil, stirring occasionally then simmer for about 5 minutes or until the peppers are reconstituted. Peel, core and dice the marrow, add to the pan. Simmer for a further 20 minutes or until the marrow is tender. Stir in the vegetable oil and serve piping hot.

SPICED PEARS

Serves Four

4 firm pears
juice of 2 lemons
grated rind of 1 lemon
1 inch cinnamon stick
4 whole cloves
pinch of salt
pinch of grated nutmeg
artificial sweetener if required

Peel the pears, cut in halves lengthwise and scoop out the core. Place in a shallow ovenproof dish, cut side upwards. Mix all the remaining ingredients together and pour them over the pears. Cover the dish and bake in a hot oven (400°F. Mark 6) for 1 hour. Serve with meat.

FRENCH BEANS VINAIGRETTE

Serves Six

1½ lb. French beans
salt
¼ teaspoon French mustard
pinch of pepper
¼ teaspoon paprika pepper
2 tablespoons vinegar
6 tablespoons vegetable oil
½ teaspoon chopped parsley
whole canned pimentoes

Prepare the beans and cook them in boiling salted water until just tender. Drain and rinse in cold water.
Mix together in a bowl ¼ teaspoon salt, French mustard, pepper, paprika pepper, vinegar, oil and chopped parsley. Whisk until well blended. Cut 6 large rings from the canned pimentoes. Place a bundle of beans in each ring. Put in a dish and pour the dressing over the top. Chill before serving.

90

Stuffed Aubergines (above)

Stuffed Onions (opposite top)

French Beans Vinaigrette (opposite bottom)

CABBAGE AND PINEAPPLE SALAD

Serves Two

½ white cabbage
½ pineapple
2 tablespoons lemon juice
artificial liquid sweetener to taste
salt and freshly ground black pepper

Shred the cabbage finely. Peel, core and chop the pineapple. Place the cabbage and the pineapple in a serving bowl, sprinkle with the lemon juice, sweetener and salt and pepper. Toss lightly to combine.
Note: 2 tablespoons of mayonnaise could be used instead of the lemon juice for a variation.

JELLIED BEETROOT SALAD

Serves One

8 fl. oz. water
1 tablespoon gelatine
juice of ½ lemon
2 tablespoons vinegar
1 tablespoon grated horse-radish
1 oz. grated onion
2 sticks celery
3 oz. cooked beetroot
3 drops artificial liquid sweetener
½ teaspoon salt
watercress for serving

Heat the water in a small saucepan, sprinkle in
the gelatine and stir until dissolved. Stir in the
lemon juice, vinegar, horse-radish and onion.
Pour into a bowl and allow to cool in the
refrigerator until almost set.
Chop the celery and beetroot. Add to the
jellied mixture with the sweetener and salt.
Pour into a wet mould and chill until set.
Arrange a bed of watercress on a serving plate
and unmould the salad on top.

COUNTRY CABBAGE

Serves Four

1 medium-sized cabbage
1 tablespoon salt
about ¼ pint water
4 sticks celery
1 red pepper
1 bunch watercress

Dressing:
6 tablespoons water
¼ pint white malt vinegar
2 teaspoons artificial liquid sweetener
1 teaspoon celery seeds

Shred the cabbage finely. Place it in a bowl in
layers, sprinkling each layer with salt and water.
Leave for 2 hours. Squeeze the cabbage to
remove the liquid.
Cut the celery into dice. Remove the seeds and
membranes from the pepper and cut into dice.
Remove the stalks from the watercress and chop.
Mix all the prepared vegetables in a bowl.
Combine all the dressing ingredients in a small
bowl, add to the vegetables and toss well.

CARROT HORS D'OEUVRE

Serves One

1 red-skinned apple
lemon juice
4 oz. carrot
4 oz. mushrooms

Sauce:
1 tablespoon mayonnaise
1 tablespoon lemon juice
1 teaspoon dried mixed herbs
½ teaspoon paprika pepper
½ teaspoon onion salt
1 teaspoon Worcestershire sauce
freshly ground black pepper to taste
artificial sweetener to taste

Chop the apple, without peeling, and toss in a
little lemon juice to prevent discoloration.
Peel and grate the carrot, wash and slice the
mushrooms thinly. Arrange the apple, carrot
and mushroom in neat rows on a serving plate.
Combine all the sauce ingredients together
thoroughly and serve in separate dish.
Chill before serving.

CUCUMBER SALAD

Serves Four

1 cucumber
1 tablespoon salt
½ teaspoon pepper
lemon juice
artificial liquid sweetener
chopped parsley for garnish

Wash the cucumber and slice thinly. Place in layers in a bowl, sprinkle each layer with salt and a little pepper. Cover the bowl and shake, gently, put aside for 15 minutes. Drain off the liquid.
Make a sweet-sour dressing by mixing lemon juice and sweetener together to taste.
Place the cucumber in a serving bowl, pour over the dressing and toss lightly. Serve garnished with chopped parsley.

HUNGARIAN PICKLED SALAD

Serves Two

4 oz. cucumber
4 oz. onion
4 oz. tomato
cider vinegar
salt and pepper

Slice all the vegetables thinly. Arrange a layer of cucumber in the bottom of a glass bowl, place onion on top and then a layer of tomato.
Pour in enough cider vinegar to cover and sprinkle with salt and pepper.
Leave for 8 hours before serving.

ORANGE AND LETTUCE SALAD

Serves One

lettuce leaves
1 medium-sized orange

Vinaigrette Dressing:
1 tablespoon vegetable oil
½ tablespoon vinegar
pinch of dry mustard
salt and pepper to taste

Shred the lettuce finely. Peel the orange, remove all the pith and skin, cut into dice.
Place the dressing ingredients in a bowl.
Whisk with a fork until thoroughly combined.
Place all the ingredients in a bowl and toss lightly all together.

NORWEGIAN COLESLAW

Serves Two

½ small white cabbage
2 inches cucumber
4 large gherkins
¼ red pepper
¼ green pepper

Dressing:
3 tablespoons lemon juice
1 tablespoon white vinegar
salt and pepper
⅛ teaspoon garlic powder (optional)
2–3 drops artificial liquid sweetener

Shred the cabbage finely. Peel the cucumber and cut in matchstick-sized pieces. Slice the gherkins thinly. Remove the seeds and membranes from the peppers. Cook them in boiling water for 5 minutes, drain and rinse in cold water.
Slice finely. Mix all the prepared vegetables in a bowl.
Place the dressing ingredients in a small screw-top jar. Shake well until thoroughly blended.
Pour the dressing over the salad and toss lightly.
Serve with poached white fish.

WINDSOR SLAW AND DRESSING

Serves Four

1 white cabbage
1 dessert apple
1 teaspoon dried onion flakes
lemon juice
cucumber
radish for garnish

Salad Dressing:
4 tablespoons mayonnaise
2 tablespoons lemon juice
3 tablespoons water
½ teaspoon salt
¼ teaspoon dry mustard
¼ teaspoon pepper

Shred the cabbage finely. Peel the apple and grate coarsely. Combine the cabbage and apple with the onion flakes and lemon juice. Line a salad bowl with thin slices of cucumber and spoon the cabbage mixture into the middle. Garnish with thin slices of radish.
Mix all the salad dressing ingredients together and serve separately.

Country Cabbage (above)

Carrot Hors d'Oeuvres (opposite top)
Marinated Mushrooms (opposite bottom)

GREEN MELODY

Serves Four

½ cucumber
6 oz. white cabbage
1 small Cos lettuce
watercress for garnish

Dressing:
2 tablespoons wine vinegar
½ teaspoon made mustard
salt and pepper
artificial sweetener to equal 1 teaspoon sugar
4 tablespoons mayonnaise

Slice the cucumber very thinly, shred the
cabbage finely, shred the lettuce. Mix the
vegetables together in a salad bowl.
Combine all the dressing ingredients together
and pour them over the salad. Toss the salad
lightly to coat in dressing. Serve garnished with
a sprig of watercress.

MARINATED MUSHROOMS

Serves Two

8 oz. mushrooms
black pepper
chopped parsley for garnish

Marinade:
½ teaspoon dry mustard
1 clove garlic, crushed
1 teaspoon artificial liquid sweetener
½ teaspoon Worcestershire sauce
¼ pint vinegar

Slice the mushrooms thinly. Whisk all the
marinade ingredients together and pour over
the mushrooms in a shallow dish. Leave for at
least 12 hours, turning frequently.
Drain the mushrooms, arrange them in a serving
dish, sprinkle with freshly ground black pepper.
Serve garnished with chopped parsley.

94

PARTY SALAD

Serves Eight

½ small white cabbage
1 red pepper
1 green pepper
8 oz. mushrooms
2 sticks celery
6 radishes
½ cucumber
½ small cauliflower
grated rind of 1 grapefruit
grated rind of 1 orange

Tomato Dressing:
6 fl. oz. wine vinegar
6 fl. oz. tomato juice
8 tablespoons vegetable oil
salt and pepper to taste
½ teaspoon dry mustard
artificial liquid sweetener to equal 1 teaspoon sugar

Shred the cabbage very finely. Remove the seeds and membranes from the peppers and slice thinly. Cut off mushroom stalks level with the caps and slice the mushrooms thinly. Chop the celery and slice the radishes and cucumber as thinly as possible. Divide the cauliflower into small flowerettes. Place the vegetables in a large bowl and combine with the grated rinds.
Mix the dressing in a small bowl, whisking well to blend thoroughly.
Toss the salad with the dressing.

FRENCH SALAD

Serves Two

1 firm head lettuce
1 clove garlic

Dressing:
½ tablespoon lemon juice
½ tablespoon tarragon vinegar
2 tablespoons vegetable oil
½ teaspoon salt
¼ teaspoon dry mustard
2 drops artificial liquid sweetener
1 teaspoon chopped parsley

Wash the lettuce and dry thoroughly. Cut the clove of garlic in half and rub round the inside of the salad bowl.
Put all the dressing ingredients in a screw-top jar and shake well until the ingredients are blended.
Pour the dressing into the salad bowl. Add the prepared lettuce and toss lightly, just before serving, to coat each leaf in the dressing.

WINTER SALAD

Serves One

4 oz. tomato
2 oz. onion
2 oz. carrot
2 oz. white cabbage
¼ green pepper

Dressing:
1 tablespoon vinegar
1 tablespoon vegetable oil
juice ¼ lemon
pinch each dried parsley, marjoram and chervil
salt and pepper

Slice the tomato thinly, grate the onion and carrot, shred the cabbage, remove the seeds and membranes from the pepper and slice thinly.
Place the dressing ingredients in a bowl and mix with a fork until thoroughly combined.
Mix the vegetables together in a bowl, add the dressing and toss to combine. Cover the bowl and put in a cool place for 2 hours before serving.

SALAD APPETIZER

Serves Four

1 can sauerkraut
2 oz. green pepper
4 oz. celery
1 tablespoon dried onion flakes
2 tablespoons artificial liquid sweetener
4 tablespoons mayonnaise
1 teaspoon Worcestershire sauce
½ teaspoon dry mustard
2 tablespoons wine vinegar
salt and pepper to taste
garlic salt (optional)

Drain the sauerkraut thoroughly. Dice the pepper and celery. Mix the sauerkraut, pepper and celery with all the other ingredients. Chill well before serving.

GREEN PEPPER AND TOMATO SALAD

Serves Four

2 green peppers
1 lb. firm red tomatoes
8 oz. spring onions
¼ teaspoon dried basil

Dressing:
1 teaspoon made mustard
salt and pepper
3 tablespoons tarragon vinegar

Slice the ends off the peppers, remove the seeds and membranes and slice into thin rings. Cut the tomatoes and spring onions into slices. Arrange all the prepared vegetables on a serving plate. Sprinkle with the basil.
Mix all the ingredients for the dressing together thoroughly. Pour over the prepared salad. Serve as soon as possible.

SEVILLE SALAD

Serves One

1 orange
2 oz. tomato
½ green pepper
2 teaspoons wine vinegar
2 teaspoons snipped chives
1 tablespoon vegetable oil
salt and pepper

Peel the orange, removing all the pith. Slice thinly, remove the pips. Immerse the tomato in boiling water for 1 minute, rinse in cold water and remove the skin. Slice. Remove the seeds and membranes from the pepper, slice thinly.

Arrange the orange and vegetables in a serving dish.
Place the vinegar, chives, oil, salt and pepper in a bowl and whisk until well blended. Pour over the salad and serve.

TOMATO PLATTER

Serves Two

6 oz. tomato
4 oz. onion

Herb Dressing:
2 tablespoons cider vinegar
2 tablespoons vegetable oil
2 teaspoons dried basil
2 tablespoons chopped parsley
1 teaspoon made mustard
grated rind of 1 lemon
salt and freshly ground black pepper
artificial sweetener to taste

Place the tomatoes in a bowl, cover with boiling water and leave for 1 minute. Rinse under cold water and peel off the skins. Slice the tomatoes thinly and arrange on a serving plate. Slice the onion thinly and place on top of the tomato.
Mix all the ingredients for the dressing together in a bowl, whisking with a fork until thoroughly combined. Pour the dressing over the tomato and onion.

Winter Salad (top p. 98)

Green Pepper and Tomato Salad (bottom p. 98)

Seville Salad (top p. 99)

Party Salad (bottom p. 99)

DESSERTS

If you are not already convinced that eating to become slim is a positive pleasure, here is a chapter that will leave you in no doubt at all. No other slimming programme in the world would let you get away with these really tempting puddings and desserts, so delicious that your slim friends will be coming back for more. Here you will find recipes for spectacular dinner party menus as well as plainer family fare.

If you are eating on your own, pamper yourself with a dessert especially made for one. Eating with your eyes is something you can still do and, indeed, are actually encouraged to do. There is nothing fattening in that. The fattening thing is your compulsion to eat the wrong foods. Make the right foods just as attractive and easy on the eye and you will find that slimming for life really is a pleasure and not a punishment.

APPLE QUEEN PUDDING Lunch

Serves One

5 tablespoons skimmed milk
artificial sweetener
1 slice white bread
1 egg, separated
1 medium-sized dessert apple

Warm the milk gently in a small saucepan.
Add 3 sweetener tablets. Crumble the bread
into an ovenproof dish, pour over the warmed
milk and leave for 10 minutes. Stir in the egg
yolk. Bake in a moderate oven (350°F. Mark 4)
for 15–20 minutes.
Peel, core and slice the apple, place in a saucepan
with 4 tablespoons water and sweetener to taste.
Simmer until tender.
Whisk the egg white with 3 crushed sweetener
tablets, until stiff.
Pour the cooked apple on to the bread and top
with the egg white. Bake in a hot oven
(400°F. Mark 6) for about 8 minutes or until
golden.

APPLE CREAM

Serves Two

2 medium-sized cooking apples
3 tablespoons low calorie lemon squash
pinch of salt
artificial sweetener to taste
1 oz. skimmed milk powder
3 tablespoons water
1 teaspoon lemon juice
½ oz. gelatine

Peel, core and slice the apples into a saucepan.
Add the squash, cover the pan and cook gently
until the apples are a dry pulp. Beat in the salt
and sweetener to taste. Mix the milk powder and
water together in a bowl and whisk until
stiffened. Press the apples through a sieve and
add to the cream with the lemon juice. Dissolve
the gelatine in 1 tablespoon very hot water,
cool. Add the gelatine to the apple mixture and
combine thoroughly.
Pour into a mould or serving dish and chill
before serving.

BAKED APPLES WITH RASPBERRIES

Serves Four

4 medium-sized cooking apples
¼ pint water
¼ teaspoon ground cinnamon
artificial sweetener
6 oz. fresh or frozen raspberries

Stand the apples firmly, stalk end downwards.
Carefully core the apples, removing the top
two-thirds only. With a sharp knife, score the
apple skin around each apple about a third of the
way down from the top. Stand the apples in a
shallow ovenproof dish.
Put the water in a saucepan with the cinnamon
and artificial sweetener to taste. Bring to the
boil, simmer for 1 minute then remove the pan
from the heat. Stir in the whole prepared
raspberries.
Carefully spoon the raspberry mixture into the
apples. Pour the remainder over the top.
Cover the dish with foil and bake in a moderate
oven (350°F. Mark 4) for 45 minutes or until
the apples are tender.

MOCK APPLE PASTRY

Serves One

1 medium-sized apple
1 teaspoon lemon juice
1 tablespoon water
¼ teaspoon ground cinnamon
artificial sweetener to equal 1 tablespoon sugar
1 slice white bread

Peel, core and slice the apple. Place the apple in
a saucepan with the lemon juice, water,
cinnamon and sweetener. Cover the pan and
cook gently until the apple is tender. Cool.
Remove the crusts from the bread and roll with
a rolling pin to make the slice thinner. Place the
apple mixture on half of the bread, fold the
bread in half diagonally and moisten the edges
to seal them together, press with a fork. Bake in
a very hot oven (425°F. Mark 7) for 15–20
minutes or until brown.

Apple Queen Pudding (p. 102)
Baked Apples Stuffed with Raspberries (p. 103)

101

APPLE AND BLACKCURRANT MOUSSE

Serves Four

1 lb. cooking apples
¼ pint low calorie blackcurrant squash
½ pint skimmed milk
3 teaspoons gelatine

Peel, core and slice the apples. Place them in a saucepan with the squash. Cover the pan, bring to the boil and simmer until the apples are tender.
Place the milk in an electric blender and blend at high speed for a few seconds. Add the apple and blackcurrant while still hot and sprinkle in the gelatine. Blend at high speed for 1 minute more.
Pour the mousse into 4 individual serving glasses and chill before serving.

APRICOT PANCAKES   Lunch

Serves One

1 egg
1 slice bread
artificial sweetener to equal 2 teaspoons sugar
2 fresh apricots
2 oz. cottage cheese
sprigs of watercress for garnish

Place the egg, bread and sweetener in an electric blender. Blend at high speed for 1 minute or until a smooth batter.
Heat a non-stick pan gently, add a little batter and cook until browned underneath. Turn and cook the other side. Continue until all the batter has been used. Stack the pancakes one on top of the other and keep warm.
Stone the apricots and chop.
Fill each pancake with some cottage cheese and apricots. Serve decorated with sprigs of watercress.

SWISS APPLE PUDDING   Lunch

Serves One

1 medium-sized apple
1 teaspoon lemon juice
4 drops vanilla essence
artificial sweetener to taste
ground cinnamon
4 fl. oz. skimmed milk
2 oz. cottage cheese
1 egg
pinch of salt
1 slice white bread

Peel the apple, core and chop finely, mix with ½ teaspoon of the lemon juice, half the vanilla essence, artificial sweetener and cinnamon to taste.
Mix the milk with the cottage cheese in a bowl. Add the egg, remaining vanilla essence and lemon juice, artificial sweetener to taste and salt.
Place the bread in the base of an ovenproof dish, cover with half of the cottage cheese mixture, top with the apple and then the remaining cottage cheese. Bake in a moderate oven (350°F. Mark 4) for about 30 minutes or until lightly browned on top.
Serve hot or cold, sprinkled with a little cinnamon.

GOOSEBERRY SORBET   Lunch

Serves Four

1 lb. green gooseberries
1 lemon
½ pint water
artificial sweetener to taste
4 eggs, separated
1 teaspoon gelatine

Top and tail the gooseberries and put into a saucepan with the grated rind of the lemon and the water. Bring to the boil, cover pan and simmer gently until the gooseberries are very soft.
Press the gooseberries through a sieve to make a purée. Put in a bowl with the lemon juice, artificial sweetener, egg yolks and the gelatine dissolved in 1 tablespoon of very hot water and cooled. Mix well. Pour into the refrigerator ice trays and place in the freezing compartment of the refrigerator until half frozen.
Beat the half frozen sorbet. Whisk the egg whites until stiff and stir in the sorbet. Return to the ice trays and freeze until firm.
Note: Turn the refrigerator to its coldest setting 1 hour before needed.

LEMON SOUFFLÉ   Lunch

Serves Two

2 lemons
¼ pint low calorie lemon squash
artificial sweetener to taste
4 teaspoons gelatine
2 eggs, separated
1 oz. skimmed milk powder

Place the lemon juice, grated rinds and lemon
squash in a saucepan with the artificial sweetener.
Add ¾ pint boiling water, sprinkle in half of the
gelatine and stir until dissolved. Allow to
partly set.
Whisk the egg yolks in a saucepan, add the milk
powder, ¼ pint water and sweetener to taste.
Heat gently without boiling, stirring until
thickened slightly. Sprinkle on the remaining
2 teaspoons gelatine and stir until dissolved.
Allow to partly set.
Whisk the partly set jelly and cream separately,
then combine the two and whisk again.
Whisk the egg whites until stiff and fold them
in to the lemon mixture. Pour into a soufflé
dish with a 'collar' of greaseproof paper coming
2 inches above the sides of the dish.
Chill, then remove the collar when set and
serve as soon as possible.

LEMON MERINGUE   Lunch

Serves Two

½ pint water
scant ½ oz. gelatine
2 eggs, separated
2 oz. breadcrumbs
1 lemon
artificial liquid sweetener to taste

Heat the water until almost boiling, sprinkle in
the gelatine and stir until dissolved. Allow to
cool then chill until beginning to set.
Put the egg yolks in a bowl, add the breadcrumbs,
grated rind and juice of the lemon and the
sweetener. Beat well. Add the lemon mixture
to the gelatine and mix thoroughly. Pour into a
cake tin and chill until set.
Whisk the egg whites until stiff and stir in
sweetener to taste. Spread on a foil-covered
baking tray to make a round. Cook in a
moderate oven (350°F. Mark 4) for about
20 minutes or until golden.
Unmould the lemon jelly on a serving plate and
top with the cooled meringue. Serve as soon as
possible.

HONEYDEW MELON SALAD

Serves Three

1 small honeydew melon
¼ cucumber
4 sticks celery
1 fresh pineapple
1 medium-sized red-skinned eating apple
2 fl. oz. unsweetened orange juice
artificial liquid sweetener
fresh mint leaves for decoration

Cut the melon in half and scoop out the flesh
with a ball-cutter, to make melon balls.
Reserve the melon skin shells. Cut the cucumber
into balls with a ball-cutter. Slice the celery
thinly. Peel and chop the pineapple. Core and
dice the apple. Combine all the prepared fruit
and vegetables in a large bowl, add the orange
juice and artificial sweetener to taste.
Spoon the salad into the reserved melon skin
shells and serve decorated with fresh mint
leaves.

Honeydew Melon Salad (p. 106)

Apple and Blackcurrant Mousse (p. 107)

LEMON STRAWBERRY FOAM

Serves Three

½ pint water
juice of 2 lemons
grated rind of 1 lemon
¾ tablespoon gelatine
artificial liquid sweetener to taste
few drops vanilla essence
2 tablespoons skimmed milk powder
15 oz. strawberries

Place the water in a saucepan with the lemon juice and rind. Bring to the boil then remove from the heat, cool slightly. Add the gelatine and stir until dissolved. Pour into a bowl and allow to become cold. Whisk in the artificial sweetener, vanilla essence and skimmed milk powder. Chill until syrupy and beginning to set. Whisk the mixture until thick and foamy, add the hulled strawberries and stir gently.
Pour the foam into a serving dish or a jelly mould, rinsed in cold water.
Unmould, if necessary, before serving.

ORANGE DELICIOUS

Serves Three

3 oranges
¼ pint water
juice of 1 lemon
artificial liquid sweetener to taste

Carefully remove the orange zest from 1 orange with a sharp knife or potato peeler, making sure not to take any of the pith. Cut the zest into matchstick strips and place them in a small saucepan with the water. Bring to the boil, simmer for 30 minutes or until tender.
Pour boiling water to cover the 3 oranges, leave for 5 minutes and then remove the oranges.
Peel, carefully removing all the pith. Slice the oranges as thinly as possible.
Place the orange slices in a serving dish. Add the lemon juice and sweetener to the orange peel water and pour it over the orange slices.
Chill thoroughly before serving.

Lemon Strawberry Foam (top p. 110)

Orange Soufflé (bottom p.110)

ORANGE SOUFFLÉ

Serves Two

scant ¾ oz. gelatine
4 fl. oz. fresh orange juice
rinds of 2 medium-sized oranges
4 fl. oz. low calorie lemon squash
1 oz. skimmed milk powder
½ teaspoon almond essence
artificial liquid sweetener to taste

Heat ¼ pint water in a small saucepan until almost boiling. Remove the pan from the heat, add ½ oz. gelatine and stir until dissolved. Pour into a measuring jug, add the orange juice and grated rind and make up to 1 pint with low calorie lemon squash and water. Chill until syrupy and beginning to set.
Dissolve the remaining scant ¼ oz. gelatine in ¼ pint water as before. Pour into a measuring jug, make up to ½ pint with cold water. Whisk in the milk powder, the almond essence and artificial liquid sweetener. Chill until syrupy and beginning to set.
Whisk the orange jelly until frothy. Whisk the almond cream until it begins to thicken. Put the two mixtures into one bowl and whisk them together until foamy and thickened. Pour the mixture into a serving bowl or a soufflé dish with a piece of double thickness greaseproof paper tied around the top to support any mixture which comes above the edge of the dish. Chill until set.
Carefully remove the greaseproof paper collar, if used, easing it away from the soufflé with the back of a knife. Serve as soon as possible.

BLACK FOREST COCKTAIL

Serves Four

2 grapefruit
2 oranges
artificial sweetener
few drops angostura bitters
few drops rum essence

Skin the fruits, cutting off all the skin and pith. With a small sharp knife, cut each fruit into segments removing all the skin.
Arrange the fruit in 4 individual serving dishes. Sprinkle each one with sweetener, angostura bitters and rum essence. Serve very cold.

FROZEN ORANGE CUPS DESSERT

Serves Four

2 teaspoons gelatine
2 tablespoons boiling water
4 oranges
6 tablespoons low calorie orange squash
mint leaves for decoration

Sprinkle the gelatine into the water and stir
until dissolved. Cut the tops off the oranges and
carefully scoop out the flesh (try using a
grapefruit knife and a spoon) without breaking
the peel. Remove the skin and place the flesh in
an electric blender. Blend at high speed with the
squash and gelatine. Alternatively, press the
orange flesh through a sieve into a bowl and
then stir in the squash and gelatine.
Pour into the refrigerator ice trays and freeze
until beginning to set around the edges. Spoon
into a bowl, beat well, then return to the
refrigerator freezing compartment until nearly
frozen. Spoon into the orange peel cups and
place in the freezing compartment again, until
needed.
Serve decorated with fresh mint leaves.
Note: Turn the refrigerator to the coldest
setting 1 hour before needed.

ITALIAN PEACHES

Serves Two

1 lemon
1 orange
½ pint water
artificial liquid sweetener to taste
1 teaspoon ground cinnamon
2 peaches

Peel the zest from the orange and lemon in
strips (a potato peeler is good for this job) and
place in a saucepan with the orange and lemon
juice, water, sweetener and cinnamon. Bring to
the boil and simmer gently for 10 minutes.
Skin the peaches by plunging them in boiling
water for 1 minute then rinsing in cold water
and peeling back the skin. Cut into slices,
remove the stones.
Arrange the peach slices in a serving dish.
Reheat the cinnamon mixture, remove the
orange and lemon strips and pour over the
peaches. Cool and then chill before serving.

PEACHES WITH STRAWBERRIES

Serves Four

4 peaches
¼ pint water
1 tablespoon lemon juice
6 drops artificial liquid sweetener
10 oz. strawberries

Wash the peaches, cut in half and remove the
stones. Heat the water in a saucepan with the
lemon juice and artificial liquid sweetener.
Add the peach halves and poach in gently
simmering water for 5 minutes. Cool.
Arrange the peach halves in a serving dish, cut
sides up. Slice the strawberries and pile in the
hollows of the peaches. Pour the cooking liquid
over the top.

PEAR IN COFFEE SAUCE

Serves One

1 medium-sized pear
1 tablespoon skimmed milk powder
1 tablespoon water
1 tablespoon strong black coffee
artificial sweetener to taste

Peel, core and slice the pear. Place it in a
saucepan with water to cover and poach gently
until the pear is tender.
Put the milk powder in a bowl with the water,
coffee and sweetener. Mix with a fork.
Drain the pears, place in a serving dish and pour
the coffee sauce over the top.
Serve warm or cold.

Tutti Frutti Mix (above)

GINGERED PINEAPPLE

Serves Four

1 fresh pineapple
1 bottle low calorie ginger ale
ground cinnamon
artificial liquid sweetener

Cut the pineapple into quarters, remove the skin
and slice. Place the slices in a shallow ovenproof
dish, pour over the ginger ale and sprinkle with
ground cinnamon and artificial liquid sweetener
to taste. Bake in a moderate oven (350°F. Mark 4)
for about 30 minutes.
Baste the pineapple with the ginger ale during
the cooking.

DAIRYMAID'S STRAWBERRIES Lunch

Serves Two

4 oz. cottage cheese
8 oz. strawberries
pinch of ground cinnamon
few drops artificial liquid sweetener (optional)
2 oz. strawberries for decoration

Place all ingredients (except the decoration) in an
electric blender and blend at high speed until
combined, about 20 seconds. Alternatively,
place all the ingredients in a bowl and mash
them very well with a fork.
Spoon the mixture into 2 serving glasses and
serve topped with fresh strawberries.

TUTTI FRUTTI MIX

Serves Two

5 oz. strawberries
1 orange
½ medium-sized pineapple
1 tablespoon lemon juice
artificial liquid sweetener (optional)

Hull the strawberries. Peel the orange removing
the pith, divide into segments cutting away all
the skin. Carefully scoop out the pineapple flesh.
Reserve the skin and cut the flesh into bite-sized
pieces. Toss all the prepared fruits in a bowl with
the lemon juice and artificial sweetener if
necessary. Pile into the reserved pineapple shell
and serve as soon as possible.

111

'MARZIPAN' STUFFED PEACH

Serves One

1 ripe peach
lemon juice
1 oz. fresh white breadcrumbs
1 tablespoon skimmed milk powder
artificial liquid sweetener to taste
almond essence to taste
water

Cut the peach in half, remove the stone and dip the cut surface in lemon juice to prevent discoloration. Place cut side up in an ovenproof dish.
Put the breadcrumbs in a bowl with the milk powder, sweetener, almond essence and enough water to bind the ingredients together. Form into a stiff paste. Divide into two and make two balls.
Place a 'marzipan' ball in each peach half.
Bake in a moderate oven (350°F. Mark 4) for 15–20 minutes. Serve hot.

FRENCH STRAWBERRY ICE

Serves One

5 oz. frozen strawberries
1 tablespoon skimmed milk powder
3 fl. oz. water
artificial liquid sweetener (optional)

Mash the strawberries in a bowl with a fork or potato masher, while still frozen. Add the other ingredients, mix well and serve at once.

LEMON MOUSSE
Lunch

Serves One

$\frac{1}{2}$ pint water
$\frac{1}{2}$ oz. gelatine
1 lemon
artificial sweetener to taste
1 egg, separated

Put the water in a saucepan, sprinkle in the gelatine and heat gently, stirring constantly, until the gelatine is dissolved. Add the lemon juice and the grated rind and allow to cool.
Strain into a bowl and stir in the sweetener and egg yolk. Chill until syrupy.
Whisk the egg white until stiff and add to the lemon jelly. Whisk the mousse altogether.
Chill until firm.

WEIGHT WATCHERS ICE CREAM
Lunch

Serves One

1 oz. skimmed milk powder
6 fl. oz. water
1 egg
artificial sweetener to taste
5 oz. strawberries

Place the milk powder, water, egg and sweetener in a bowl and whisk well, preferably with an electric mixer, until frothy. Place in the refrigerator ice trays and put into the freezing compartment until beginning to set around the edges. Return the ice cream to the bowl and whisk again until thick and smooth. Freeze again as before then whisk again.
Pour the ice cream back into ice trays and freeze until firm. Serve when needed, with the strawberries.
Note: Turn the refrigerator to its coldest setting 1 hour before needed.

POOR KNIGHTS

Serves One

1 slice white bread
skimmed milk
2 slices pineapple
ground cinnamon
artificial sweetener (optional)

Place the bread in a shallow dish, cover with milk and leave until the bread is saturated.
Place the bread about 3 inches from a hot grill and cook until golden, turning once. Place on a hot serving plate.
Place the pineapple under the grill, sprinkle with a little cinnamon and sweetener if liked. Grill until hot.
Place the pineapple on the bread and serve.

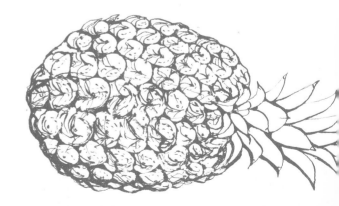

RHUBARB FOOL

Serves Two

1 lb. rhubarb
18 drops artificial liquid sweetener
2 eggs
6 fl. oz. skimmed milk
2 slices lemon for decoration

Cut the rhubarb into 2 inch lengths and place it in a saucepan with 2 tablespoons water and 10 drops of artificial sweetener. Cover the pan and cook very gently until tender. Cool and then press through a sieve or blend in an electric blender until smooth.
Beat the eggs, warm the milk and mix the two together with the remaining 8 drops sweetener. Strain the egg mixture into a saucepan and heat very gently, stirring constantly until thickened. Mix the egg custard with the rhubarb and chill. Spoon into individual serving glasses and decorate with a slice of lemon.

FRUIT FOOL

Serves One

3 oz. gooseberries, blackberries, black or red currants
3 tablespoons water
artificial liquid sweetener to equal 3 teaspoons sugar
½ oz. skimmed milk powder

Top and tail the gooseberries and put into a saucepan with 2 tablespoons water. Cover the pan and cook gently until the fruit is soft. Place in an electric blender and blend at high speed until smooth then press through a sieve. Place in a bowl, stir in the sweetener.
Mix the milk powder with the remaining 1 tablespoon water and whisk it into the gooseberry purée.
Chill before serving.

STRAWBERRY ALASKA

Serves Two

1 teaspoon gelatine
6 tablespoons skimmed milk powder
1 teaspoon vanilla essence
artificial sweetener to taste
2 eggs, separated
10 oz. strawberries

Dissolve the gelatine in 1 tablespoon very hot water, cool. Place the gelatine in a bowl with 6 fl. oz. water, the milk powder, vanilla essence and sweetener to taste. Whisk well until stiff. Stir in the egg yolks and the strawberries. Pour the mixture into the refrigerator ice trays and place in the freezing compartment until frozen hard.
Whisk the egg whites until stiff, fold in sweetener to taste.
Place the frozen ice cream on an ovenproof dish. Cover it completely with the whisked egg whites, making sure that it comes right to the edge of the dish all the way round. Bake in a very hot oven (475°F. Mark 9) until golden, 2–3 minutes.
Serve immediately.

FRUIT TART WITH 'SPOIL YOURSELF' CREAM

Serves One

1 slice bread
juice of 1 lemon
1 medium-sized cooking apple
artificial sweetener
1 teaspoon gelatine
1 egg, separated
1 tablespoon skimmed milk powder

Roll out the bread with a rolling pin until thin. Line a plate with the bread and sprinkle with lemon juice.
Cook the apple in a covered saucepan with ¼ pint water and artificial sweetener if necessary, until just tender. Drain the apple and place on the bread. Measure the liquid and make up to ¼ pint with hot water if necessary. Sprinkle in the gelatine and stir until dissolved. Put juice in a cool place until syrupy and almost set. Stir in the egg yolk and pour over the fruit.
Whisk the egg white until stiff, add the milk powder and artificial sweetener to taste slowly, whisking well all the time.
Pile the 'cream' on to the fruit and serve.

COTTAGE CHEESECAKE — Lunch

Serves Four

4 slices bread
8 oz. cottage cheese
4 eggs
½ pint skimmed milk
artificial liquid sweetener to equal 2 tablespoons
sugar
1 lemon

Bake the bread in a very hot oven (450°F.
Mark 8) until golden brown. Crush the bread
with a rolling pin to make it into crumbs.
Spread them into the base of an 8 inch
spring-form tin.
Rub the cottage cheese through a metal sieve or
beat in an electric mixer at a very high speed.
Add the eggs, milk, artificial sweetener and the
finely grated rind and the juice of the lemon.
Mix thoroughly. When smooth, pour the cheese
mixture onto the crumbs in the cake tin. Bake in
a moderate oven (350°F. Mark 4) for 30–40
minutes or until set.
Place the cheesecake in the refrigerator and
chill overnight.
Remove from the tin and serve.

SWEDISH SPRITS — Lunch

Serves One

1 oz. fine white breadcrumbs
1 tablespoon skimmed milk powder
1 egg
½ teaspoon vanilla essence
½ teaspoon artificial liquid sweetener

Place all the ingredients in a bowl and blend
them together thoroughly. Leave the mixture to
stand for 10 minutes.
Spoon the mixture in to a piping bag with a
large star piping tube. Pipe rosettes onto a
foil-covered baking tray. Place under a
moderately hot grill and cook gently for about
30 minutes or until golden brown.
Serve hot or cold.

TOASTED CINNAMON SLICE

Serves One

1 oz. slice of bread
1 tablespoon skimmed milk powder
2 teaspoons warm water
3 drops almond essence
3 drops artificial liquid sweetener
½ teaspoon ground cinnamon
1 slice of lemon for decoration

Cut the bread into three 1 inch fingers. Mix all
the remaining ingredients together, except the
decoration, combine thoroughly. Brush the
bread fingers with the cinnamon mixture and
layer them one on top of the other. Secure with
2 wooden cocktail sticks. Bake in a hot oven
(400°F. Mark 6) for 10–15 minutes.
Serve decorated with a slice of lemon.

FLOATING ISLANDS — Lunch

Serves Two

½ pint skimmed milk
¼ teaspoon grated nutmeg
2 eggs, separated
artificial sweetener to taste
vanilla essence
¾ tablespoon gelatine

Put the milk and nutmeg into a large saucepan
or a frying pan. Whisk the egg white until
stiff, add sweetener to taste.
Heat the milk and, when simmering, drop in
2 or 3 teaspoons of meringue. Cook for 3–4
minutes, turning once. Remove with a slotted
spoon and drain on a clean tea towel or absorbent
kitchen paper. Continue in this way until all the
meringue is cooked.
Allow the milk to cool then whisk in the egg
yolk. Sprinkle in the gelatine and stir until
dissolved, add the vanilla essence. Strain the egg
custard into a serving dish and float the meringue
'islands' on top. Chill until set.

Floating Islands (opposite)

114

DRINKS

You'll be surprised just how many delicious drinks you can make and still be happy in the knowledge that you are doing nothing to make yourself fat. The children will be pestering you to make some for them, too, especially those creamy looking sodas and shakes. Here you will find long refreshing drinks for summer days as well as non-alcoholic cocktails, sophisticated enough to serve up at the smartest of parties. Treat yourself to some elegant new glasses and serve up the drinks so that they look as good as you know they taste.

APRICOT FLIP

Serves Four

1 lb. fresh apricots
¼ pint water
artificial sweetener to taste
3 pints skimmed milk

Put the apricots and water into a saucepan with
sweetener to taste. Bring to the boil, cover the
pan and simmer until the apricots are very
tender. Remove the stones.
Pour the apricots and the milk into an electric
blender. Blend at high speed until frothy. Pour
into 4 glasses and serve immediately.

MINT DEWLIP

Serves Four

2 tablespoons chopped mint leaves
artificial sweetener to equal 1 oz. sugar
1½ pints Slimline ginger ale
ice cubes

Mix the mint leaves with the sweetener in a
large jug. Pour in the ginger ale and allow to
stand for at least 30 minutes.
Put ice cubes in the bottom of 4 tall glasses and
pour the mint dewlip over the top. Serve as
soon as possible.

GOOSEBERRY REFRESHER

Serves Four

1 lb. ripe gooseberries
1 large lemon
artificial sweetener to taste
1½ pints water
½ pint soda water

Put the gooseberries into a saucepan with the
sliced lemon, artificial sweetener and the water.
Bring to the boil, cover the pan and simmer
gently until the gooseberries are tender. Remove
from the heat and cool.
Pour the liquid from the gooseberries into 4 tall
glasses and add ¼ of the soda water to each.
Serve decorated with the gooseberries divided
into four equal portions.

GRAPEFRUIT FIZZ

Serves Two

4 ice cubes
8 oz. unsweetened grapefruit juice
1 bottle soda water
slices of lemon

Crush ice cubes and divide between 2 tall
glasses. Add grapefruit juice and top up with
soda water. Serve at once with lemon slices
floating on top.

117

THREE FRUIT CUP

Serves Two

½ pint Slimline sparkling orange
¼ pint Slimline bitter lemon
10 oz. strawberries
cucumber for garnish
crushed ice

Pour the orange and the lemon into a jug and
mix. Cut the strawberries in half and slice the
cucumber as thinly as possible.
Place the crushed ice in the base of a chilled
glass jug, pour the mixed orange and lemon over
the top and add the strawberries and cucumber.
Serve immediately.

COCKTAIL REFRESHER

Serves Four

¾ pint tomato juice
1 small stick celery, with leaves
2 tablespoons parsley sprigs
2 slices lemon
1 teaspoon dried onion flakes
¼ teaspoon salt
few drops artificial liquid sweetener (optional)

Place all the ingredients in an electric blender
and blend at high speed until smooth. Allow to
stand for 20 minutes.
Serve in tall glasses.

STRAWBERRY MILK SHAKE

Serves One

2 oz. skimmed milk powder
5 oz. strawberries
about 16 drops artificial liquid sweetener
4 drops vanilla essence
½ pint cold water
slice of orange or a strawberry for decoration

Place all the ingredients in an electric blender.
Blend at high speed until smooth.
Pour the milk shake into a glass and chill.
Serve decorated with a twist of orange or a
strawberry.

ICED COFFEE

Serves One

2 tablespoons skimmed milk powder
1 tablespoon cold water
3–4 drops artificial liquid sweetener
crushed ice
¼ pint cold black coffee
grated nutmeg

Put the milk powder in a bowl with the water
and liquid sweetener. Whisk well. Put some
crushed ice in the base of a tall glass, add the
sweetened milk and finally the black coffee.
Serve as soon as possible, sprinkled with a little
grated nutmeg.

Strawberry Milk Shake (p. 118)

Iced Coffee (p. 119)

JAMAICA ORANGE

Serves One

4 fl. oz. Slimline sparkling orange
about ½ teaspoon rum essence
twist of lemon peel and ice for serving

Pour the orange into a glass, stir in the rum
essence. Serve with ice, decorated with a twist
of lemon peel.

SATIN SLIPPER

Serves One

4 tablespoons low calorie bitter lemon
6 tablespoons tomato juice
1 teaspoon lemon juice
1–2 chopped mint leaves

Chill all the ingredients well then mix them
and serve.

PARTY MENUS

Once you are slim, entertaining is something you will certainly want to do. In this chapter you will see just how easy it is to entertain your friends with the food *you* enjoy. Here are recipes for all sorts of party-giving occasions, Christmas lunch, Boxing Day dinner, and a special summer lunch, too. Not only will your friends enjoy eating them, they will never believe you were all eating to keep slim.

CHRISTMAS DAY LUNCHEON

LEMON ARTICHOKES

Serves Four

2 cloves garlic, crushed
4 tablespoons lemon juice
2 tablespoons dried onion flakes
1 tablespoon dried oregano
16 oz. artichoke hearts
1 pint chicken stock made with chicken stock cube and water
salt and pepper to taste
parsley pats, see below

Combine garlic, lemon juice, onion flakes, oregano and chicken stock together in saucepan. Bring to the boil and simmer until the onion is softened. Add the artichokes and heat through. Drain the artichokes and serve them with the parsley pats.
Note: The liquid from this dish makes a delicious clear soup.

Parsley Pats
2 oz. vegetable margarine
4 teaspoons lemon juice
4 teaspoons dried parsley

Mix all the ingredients together thoroughly in a small bowl. Form into 4 pats on plate and chill thoroughly.

Christmas Day Luncheon (p. 122)

ROAST BEEF PIQUANT
Lunch

Serves Eight

$1 \times 3\frac{1}{2}$ lb. beef sirloin
2 teaspoons salt
$\frac{3}{4}$ teaspoon pepper
1 teaspoon paprika pepper
2 cloves garlic, crushed
$\frac{1}{2}$ pint wine vinegar
$\frac{1}{2}$ pint water

Season the meat with salt, pepper, paprika and garlic. Marinate the meat in a mixture of vinegar and water. Place in the refrigerator overnight. Drain. Place the meat on a rack in a roasting pan. Roast uncovered in moderate oven (350°F. Mark 4) until tender, (20–22 minutes per lb. for medium cooked).
Serve with Brussels sprouts and jacket potatoes.

BANANA AND LEMON MOUSSE

Serves Four

$2\frac{1}{2}$ tablespoons gelatine
8 fl. oz. water
16 fl. oz. low calorie lemon squash
4 oz. skimmed milk powder
4 bananas

Dissolve gelatine in the water in a bowl over a saucepan of simmering water. Add the low calorie squash. Slowly add the skimmed milk powder and whisk well. Mash the banana with a fork and beat all together until smooth. Pour into a mould and allow to set in a cool place.

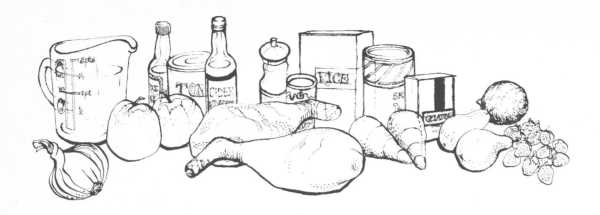

BOXING DAY DINNER

FRENCH ONION SOUP

Serves Four

1½ pints water
3 beef stock cubes
8 oz. sliced onions
1½ teaspoons Worcestershire sauce
½ teaspoon Aromat
black pepper

Place all the ingredients in a saucepan and bring to the boil. Cover the pan and simmer until the onion is tender, approximately 30 minutes.

CURRY AND RICE   Dinner

Serves Four

4 oz. chopped onion
4 oz. finely diced carrot
2 cooking apples
12 fl. oz. tomato juice
½ pint chicken stock made with chicken stock cube and water
2 tablespoons cider vinegar
1½ lb. cooked turkey, chicken, beef or lamb
salt and pepper to taste
few drops artificial liquid sweetener
2 teaspoons curry powder or to taste
12 oz. cooked rice

Place the onion, carrot, peeled, cored and diced apples, tomato juice, chicken stock, cider vinegar and salt and pepper together in a saucepan. Bring to boil and simmer until tender. Add the chopped poultry or meat, liquid sweetener and curry powder and simmer for 5 minutes.
Serve with hot freshly-cooked rice.

ROSY PEAR CHIFFON

Serves Four

2 pears
½ pint water
½ tablespoon lemon juice
artificial liquid sweetener to taste
10 oz. strawberries
1 tablespoon gelatine
2 oz. skimmed milk powder

Halve and core the pears and place in a saucepan with the water, lemon juice and liquid sweetener. Simmer, covered, for about 10 minutes or until the pears are tender. Drain and reserve the liquid. Mash the strawberries. Make up liquid from pears with water to 12 fl. oz. Soften gelatine in 2 fl. oz. hot water, stir until dissolved. Add to the strawberry mixture with liquid sweetener. Chill in the refrigerator until the mixture is syrupy. Coarsely chop the pears, fold into the gelatine mixture. Combine skimmed milk powder with 2 fl. oz. iced water. Whisk at high speed in an electric mixer until mixture stands in peaks. Fold into gelatine mixture.
Spoon into 4 dessert bowls and allow to set.

SUMMER DAYS LUNCH

GRAPE SALAD

Serves Four

1½ lb. green grapes
4 tablespoons gelatine
juice of 4 lemons
water
4 teaspoons chopped mint
artificial sweetener to taste
green colouring
lettuce for serving

Peel and pip grapes. Dissolve gelatine in little water in a bowl over a saucepan of simmering water. Add the strained lemon juice, enough water to make up 2 pints liquid, chopped mint, sweetener and colouring. Chill. When on point of setting, add the grapes. Pour into 4 moulds. Turn out and serve with crisp lettuce.

SEAFOOD SALAD MOULD   Lunch

Serves Four

2 tablespoons gelatine
16 fl. oz. water
2 lemons
½ teaspoon salt
1 teaspoon Worcestershire sauce
1–2 drops Tabasco sauce
1 lb. shrimps or prawns
4 sticks celery
1 green pepper
4 oz. finely chopped spring onions
2 tomatoes
green salad
4 tablespoons mayonnaise

Soften the gelatine in 4 fl. oz. cold water. Add 8 fl. oz. boiling water and stir until gelatine is dissolved. Stir in the remaining cold water, grated rind and juice of the lemons, salt, Worcestershire sauce and Tabasco sauce. Pour a thin layer of gelatine mixture into 2½ pint mould and arrange shrimps or prawns in it. Chill until set. Chill remaining gelatine mixture until slightly thickened then fold in finely chopped celery, pepper, spring onions and tomato, skinned. Carefully pour over shrimps or prawns. Chill until firm. Unmould and serve with green salad and mayonnaise.

INSTANT ORANGE ICE CREAM

Serves Four

2 oranges
2 oz. skimmed milk powder
½ teaspoon artificial liquid sweetener
½ teaspoon vanilla essence
12–16 ice cubes
4 sprigs fresh mint

Peel, quarter and remove the seeds from the oranges. Combine all the ingredients, except the mint sprigs in an electric blender and blend until smooth and creamy.
Pour into well chilled dessert glasses and garnish with mint.
Serve at once.
Note: This ice cream will keep up to 12 hours in freezer compartment of refrigerator.

INDEX

All recipes have been indexed according to the meal at which they may be eaten.